WILTON
THROUGH TIME
Chris Rousell

AMBERLEY PUBLISHING

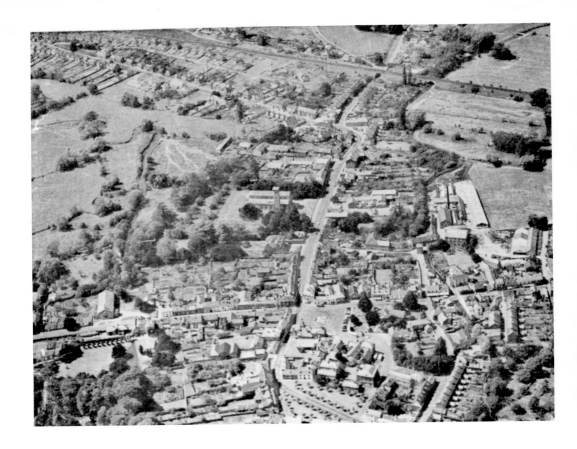

First published 2010

Amberley Publishing Plc
Cirencester Road, Chalford,
Stroud, Gloucestershire, GL6 8PE

www.amberley-books.com

ISBN 978 1 84868 401 0

British Library Cataloguing in Publication Data.
A catalogue record for this book is available from
the British Library.

Typeset in 9.5pt on 12pt Celeste.
Typesetting by Amberley Publishing.
Printed in the UK.

Introduction

The market town of Wilton which has a long and cherished history, is situated three miles west of Salisbury, nestling at the head of the Wylye and Nadder valleys, their respective rivers flowing through the town, which is reputed to be the second oldest Borough in the country. The roots of the town were firmly established as far back to around the middle of the sixth century. First settlers, who found conditions here very much to their liking, were a tribe of Saxons who became known locally as the 'Wil-Sateas' this being loosely interpreted as "Dwellers who came to live on the banks of rivers with many willow trees".

It was these rivers on either side in the west and the east, which formed natural boundaries, as did the downlands at the northern end, where at that time the woods, known today as Groveley Woods, stretched right down to the area we know today as St. John's Square. At the more vulnerable southern end, strong balustrades were constructed as a form of defence. It is intriguing to note, that one of the earliest maps of the town, showing the area used by the Saxon settlers, reveals that the main part of the town is practically the same layout which is still in existence today.

The settlement soon grew, eventually establishing itself as one of the places which the Kings of Wessex would stop off at as they travelled through their kingdom. It was due to this practice that Wilton became established as a capitol town in Wessex. After the Danes were defeated by King Alfred here in Wilton, the town took on the role of becoming an important religious centre, dominated by an Abbey. It was here that Saxon Princesses and daughters of noblemen received their education. One of these ladies was Edith, the daughter of King Edgar and the Abbess, Wulfrith. Edith devoted her life to God, becoming skilled in many occupations, but at the age of twenty-three, she caught a fever and passed away. Not long after her tragic death, she was canonised, and today she is the town's Patron Saint.

The Abbey existed for many years; travellers spent the night within its walls. However, with the dissolution of such buildings being ordered by Henry VIII, Wilton Abbey, along with the extensive lands it owned, which included those on the Isle of Wight, were given by King Henry, to the Earl of Pembroke. He demolished the Abbey, using most of its stone, to build Wilton House on the site, which to this day, is still the family seat of the Pembroke family.

Wilton has been fortunate in its associations with royalty, this being shown by the town having been granted no less than fifteen Royal Charters by various kings. The first one was dated 1100, granted by Henry I, and the last one by Queen Victoria in 1885. This charter was important, with the borough boundary being extended. Due to these changes, a new Corporation was elected, this format of local government remaining in force in the town, until the local government changes instigated by Parliament in 1974. This led to Wilton losing its borough status, but it kept its Mayor, allowing a tradition dating from 1265.

In its early years, Wilton enjoyed great economic importance, when markets and fairs flourished, drawing in people from all round the district, plus other places further afield. There were a wide variety of crafts that were active, including weaving, brewing, baking, needle making and many more.

Unfortunately, the growth of New Salisbury ended Wilton's prosperity, leading to the town falling into decline and decay, lasting over a long period of years. The only real survivor was the textile industry, in particular, weaving. Fortunately, during the early eighteenth century, prosperity started to return, and with the birth of the carpet making industry, this was to determine the salvation of the town. Later, felt making was also able to contribute to the prosperity, with the establishment of a mill in Crow Lane. Prosperity was further enhanced with the arrival of the railway, the first company being the Great Western Railway, operating a service through the Wylye Valley to Bristol. Three years later, in 1859, the London and South Western Railway, commenced their service from Salisbury to Gillingham, which was later extended to Exeter.

Despite this prosperity, there was a large community of poor people, whose survival relied on assistance with regular payments from 'the poor relief fund', which was set up by various benefactors in the town. It was these people who, between them, provided help and assistance from the cradle to the grave. Another benefactor provided education for twenty poor boys of the parish. Girls were not left out, when a Dame School was provided in the grounds of Wilton Park. Eventually a National School was provided in West Street, which still stands today, serving as the town's Community Centre.

The twentieth century was destined to endure two World Wars, with the inhabitants of Wilton becoming heavily involved in both of them, in various ways. During the First World War, they played host to many Australian soldiers who visited the town, when they had time off from training in the many camps that had sprung up on Salisbury Plain, as well as some villages in the Wylye and Nadder Valleys. Many a friendship was made on these occasions, my own family included.

During the Second World War, many inhabitants took in evacuees who had arrived here from the Portsmouth area, for the duration. Later, American troops arrived, and they established a camp up the Avenue. They also established an ammunition store in Grovely Woods, which put the woods 'out of bounds' to the public until after the war had ceased. The ammunition was used for the D-Day operation.

Although in early times, some drawings and sketches were made of the town; they were few and far between, and not always accurate, but with the advent of the camera and the photograph, a new form of illustrating history was born. One very popular way of recording visual history, was made popular through the humble postcard, of which thousands were produced in this country. Not only with architecture of street scenes, images of the residents caught on camera, throughout the passing years, reveal the changing vogue in fashion throughout the years to the present day.

One particular prolific cameraman in Wilton was William Jukes, who owned a printing works in North Street, which was situated in a building immediately opposite where the post office stands today. He spent many hours going about the town with his camera mounted on a tripod, taking photographs of many locations around the town, which were produced on his glass negatives. From these he turned out many postcards, eagerly bought by tourists of the day, as well as residents, who on many occasions sent them when communicating with relatives or friends. Even my grandfather, William James Lane, who was a Wilton correspondent for the *Salisbury Journal*, also recorded scenes with his camera. Other postcard manufacturers also came to Wilton recording scenes in the town, today which reveal many scenes and buildings from a bygone era, which will never return, but will live on having been preserved in different forms of archival formats.

But what about today; who is recording the scenes of the more present day ever-changing scenes? In the late 1990s, the late Bill Cannings went on a wander round the town with his camera, recording street scenes, buildings and some special events, some of these appearing in this book. I have continued in his footsteps, and on the last day of the twentieth century, I photographed the street scenes on the last day of the twentieth century, so at least there is a record of how Wilton looked on that unique day in history. It was one of those 'once in a lifetime' moments that just had to be recorded, which is solely made possible with the aid of the camera.

Chris Rousell
Wilton, 2010

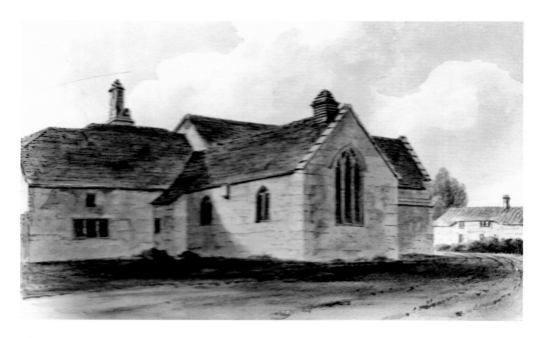

The Priory Church

The Priory Church, also known as the Hospital of St. John, situated at the far end of West Street, which was founded by Bishop Hubert Walter, Bishop of Sarum in the reign of Richard I. The original foundation was for a priory supporting two poor women, and at the time of the Reformation was considered more a charitable venture than a religious one and was therefore not dissolved. The above illustration shows approximately how the church looked in the late twelfth/thirteenth centuries. Today the church stands on the corner of the busy A36 main road. A regular communion service is still held here once a week, and the charitable status is still available under the Wilton Charities.

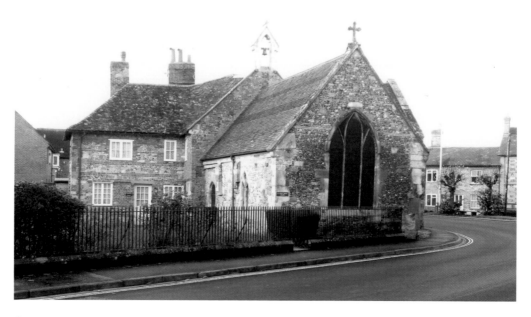

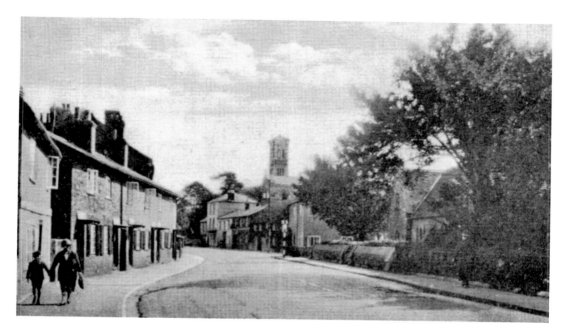

West Street 1930s

Looking down West Street in what are probably the late 1930s shows a time when there was not much traffic on the roads. The house to the right at the end of the wall was the Toll House, which at this time was not in commission. The almshouses can just be made out between the trees, these still being in use today, as rented properties. As one can see in the picture below, taken in 2009, there have been quite a few changes that have taken place; the Toll House had disappeared, along with the row of cottages on the left hand side. However, the Parish Church still continues to dominate the scene to this day. The photograph below shows a very different view.

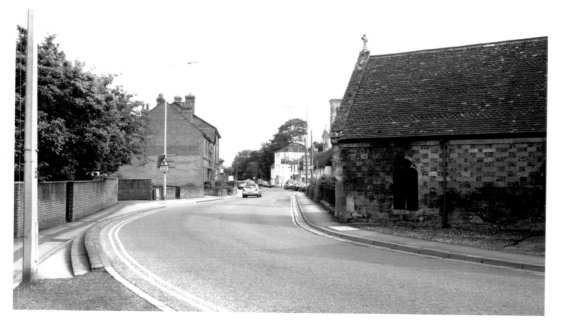

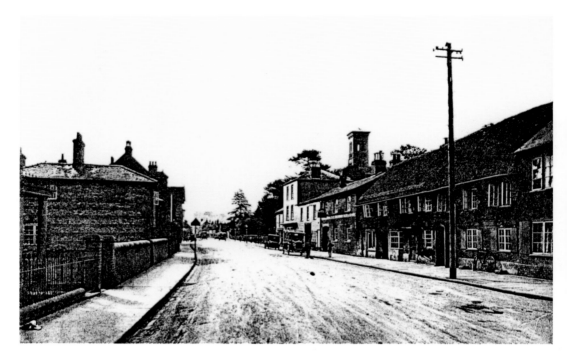

West Street 1900s/1920s

Another scene of West Street thought to have been taken in the late 1900s/early 1920s. The low wall on the left has behind it a large yard, where Brewers the agriculturists kept their tractors on sale, and in later years, combine harvesters. The yard is still in operation today, but the firm carrying the same trade in the sale of tractors established by Brewers, is A. J. Cole of Blandford. Changes have taken place beyond the wall further down the street.

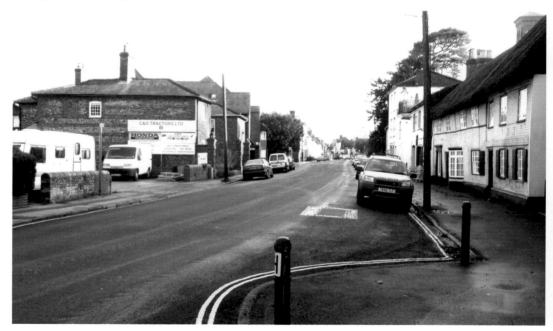

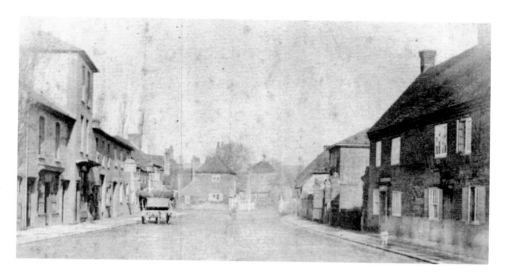

West Street c. 1875

This view is looking towards the location from where the previous picture was taken. The one above is reputed to be the oldest photograph of West Street taken *c.* 1875, which shows the Old Toll Gate actually in position. This print was taken from the original glass negative at a later date, but unfortunately the negative had been incorrectly stored and had become damaged, which unfortunately shows on the sepia print above. The row of cottages on the right; were replaced in the late 1990s with Pembroke Court sheltered houses for the elderly, which can be clearly seen on the right in the photograph below.

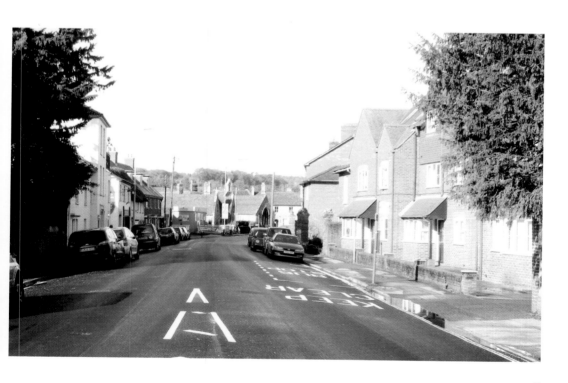

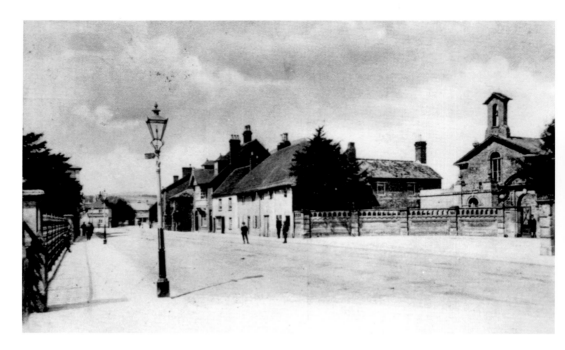

The National School

An early tinted colour postcard of West Street, showing the National School. Originally a mill, it became a parochial school, then a day school in 1842, united with the National Society in 1902. The picture was obviously taken in the early 1900s, as the road surface is made up of compacted earth. It is also in the period of gas lighting of the streets, with the gas being supplied by the Wilton Gas Works, who were situated up the Kingsway, on the left hand side, just before the GWR road bridge. The actual building is still *in situ*, in use as a garage and M.O.T. inspection centre.

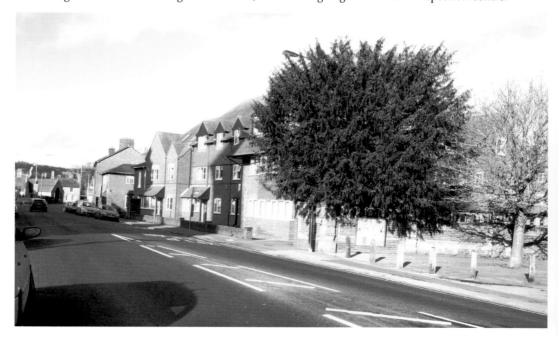

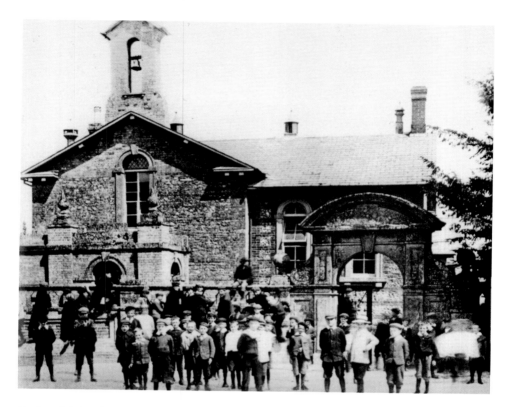

National School Pupils, 1907

Pupils outside the National School entrance, 1907. The Archway was long demolished, as was the attached building seen over the wall on the left. Also, another loss is the structure which housed the school bell. Most of the original façade still remains and in 1975 the building reopened, becoming the town's Community Centre.

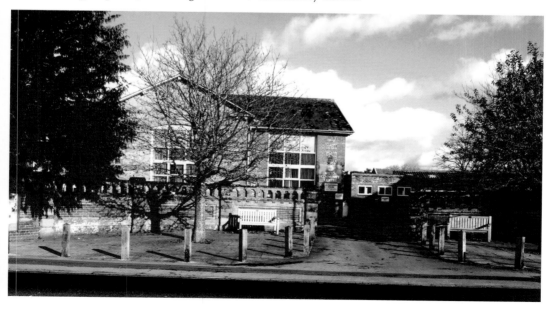

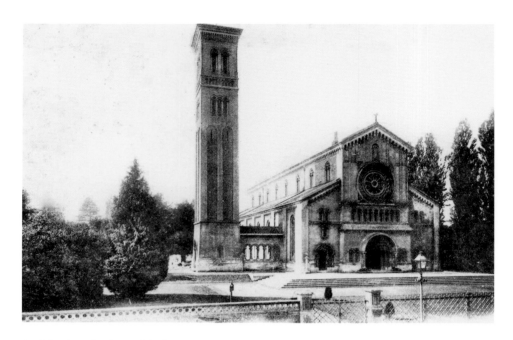

Parish Church of St Nicholas

This postcard of the Parish Church of St Nicholas was produced by William Jukes of Wilton. The photograph was taken not long after its opening, which is made more interesting, because William Jukes seemed to be, at this period in time, experimenting with colour tinting. The church was built to replace the former Parish Church of St Mary in the Market Square, which was falling badly into a state of disrepair. The Church which was gift to the town by Sidney Herbert, who had the church styled on the Lombardic churches of St. Pitero and Santa Maria which stand in northern Rome outside Tuscania, near Viterbo, which is especially noticeable in the interior design. The church was consecrated by Bishop Denison of Salisbury 9 October 1845.

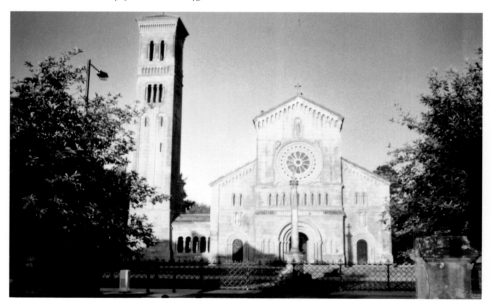

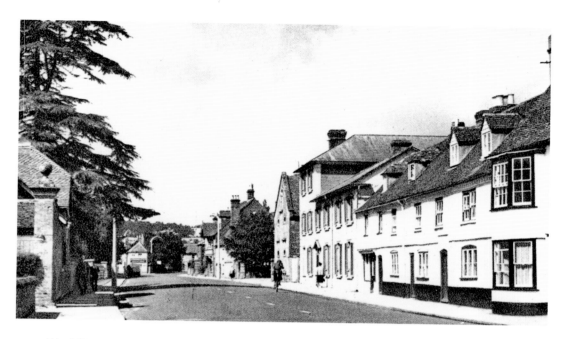

West Street 1940s

West Street, the main thoroughfare through the town, on what today is the A30 to Devon and Cornwall, is practically deserted in this late 1940s street scene. The only signs of life being a lone cyclist, two ladies on the right-hand pavement and two gentlemen in the shadows on the left. The same view over half a century later, below, reveals a vast difference. Now the Priory Church and the trees on the downs at the northern end of the town are all now clearly visible. The age of the car now dominates the former peacefulness of the street scene, as does the modern day street furniture of modern style street lamps and telephone poles.

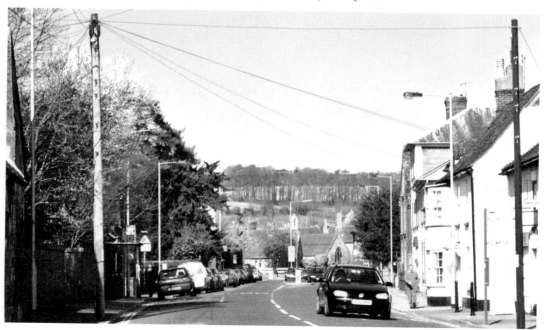

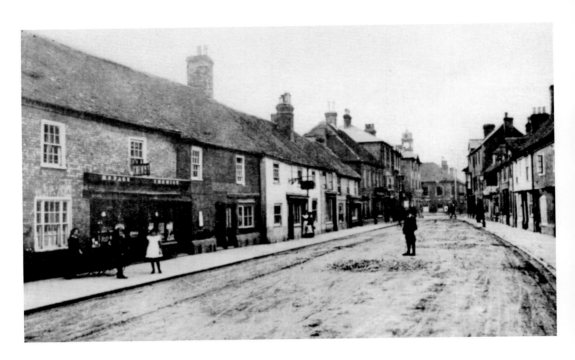

West Street 1915

The picture above taken was taken in West Street during the First World War in 1915. It would appear the photographer has attracted a lot of attention, judging by the number of Wiltonians standing there watching the photographer at work. Below, ninety-four years later, this photograph taken on a Sunday morning in May 2009, shows that as far as the buildings go, very little has changed in the intervening years. At the time the road surface was in a bad state of repair, but the dirt road above doesn't appear to have a pothole in sight.

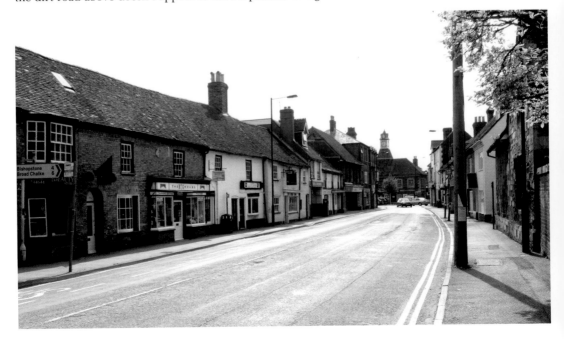

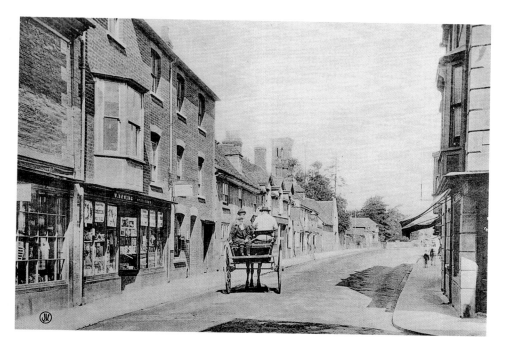

North Street into West Street

A real step back in time when life was run at a more leisurely pace. The horse cart has just turned out of North Street into West Street. Unfortunately, no date is given, but at the time Mr Boning was in business as a newsagent and stationer, his shop always was a very busy one. He was also noted for selling many postcards of the town, many of which can still be purchased at specialist outlets, bearing his shop name. Today the business has completely changed to a chiropractor's. Below shows the same scene photographed at 6am on a July morning in 2004, before the traffic builds up for the day.

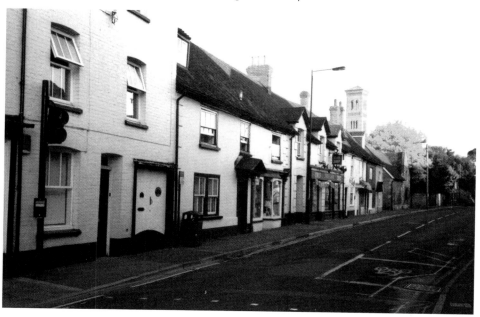

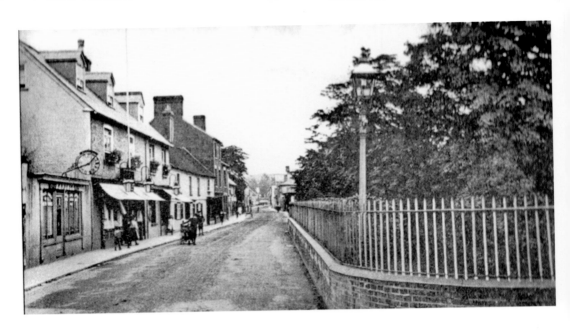

North Street early 1900s

The shop on the left is possibly a clockmaker and repairer. The shop next to it was Joseph Ward's drapery business in which he employed his two daughters Mary and June as shop assistants. In later times it became a branch of Barclays Bank, before it closed around 2006/7. The railings surrounding the churchyard of St Mary's Church were removed between January and July 1940, for a wartime scrap metal drive. Below shows the same scene taken by myself on the last day of the twentieth century. Unfortunately, weather-wise it was a rather dull and misty day, which shows up well in the photograph, capturing that day exactly as it was.

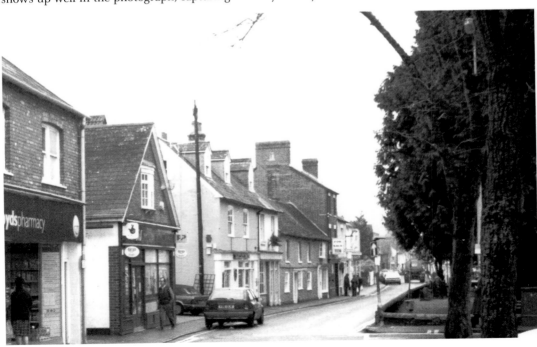

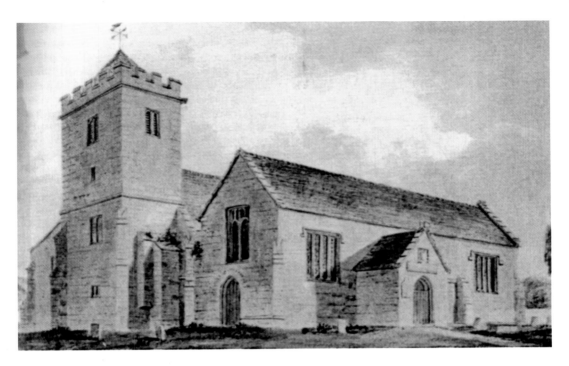

Parish Church of St Mary in the Market Place

The illustration above shows, with good accuracy, exactly how the former Parish Church of St Mary in the Market Place looked not long after it was built. Note the houses opposite the church in North Street were *in situ* at this time. Below is the view of how the ruins compare today with the above sketch. Many of the grave headstones have also been moved for safety purposes.

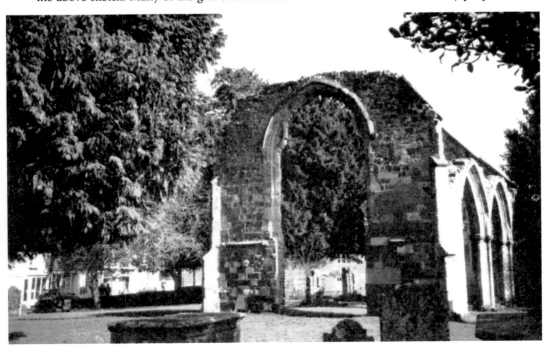

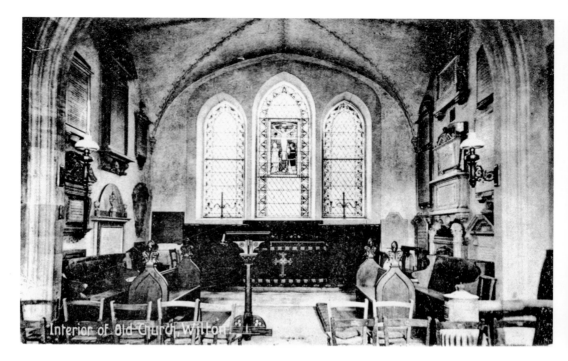

Interior of Old Church, Wilton

William Jukes of Wilton

Above is a photograph taken by William Jukes of Wilton, who owned a printing business in North Street. This was one of many which he reproduced as postcards in the early 1900s. Up until 1845, this was the parish church of the town, until it was replaced by the present one, due to it falling into a state of disrepair. Changes have taken place in the one taken in 1997; although the church is now classed as redundant, it still remains as a consecrated building and occasional services can still be held if the need arises.

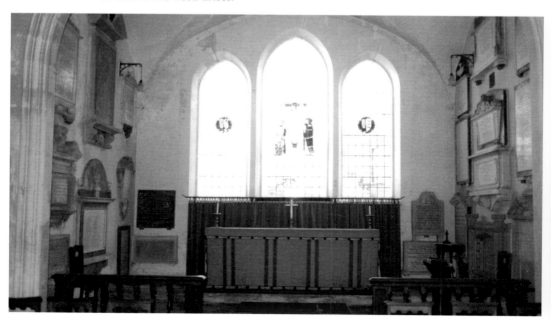

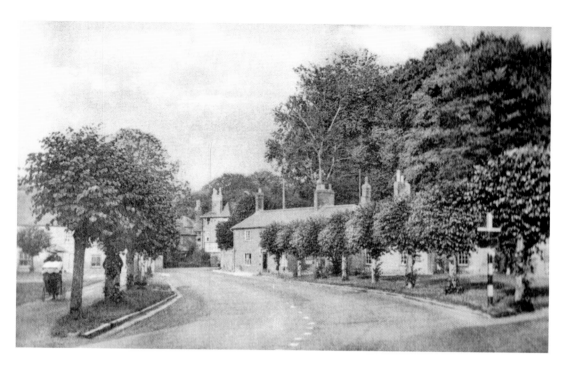

Kingsbury Square

Kingsbury Square is one of the few places in the town which has changed very little over the years. Unfortunately there is no date for the photograph above, which could possibly be late 1900s to early 1920s. The name Kingsbury means 'The Stronghold of the King'. It is thought that the Kings of Wessex, when they travelled through their Kingdom, had a palace nearby, or possibly somewhere inside this area.

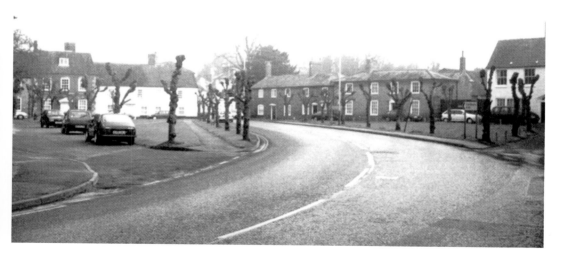

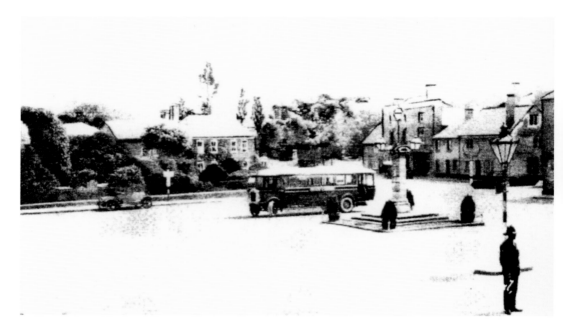

The Market Place

Buses still use the Market Place as a bus stop today, but much has changed since the photograph above was taken in the late 1920s. The old Co-op building behind Sidney Herbert's Memorial and the cottages were demolished in the late 1970s and replaced by the Wilton Health Centre. Later the Sidney Herbert Memorial was removed to make way for a centre of town car park. In the late 1970s an enhancement scheme was put in place with trees lining three sides, with the central area still being used for car parking. The photograph below was taken in June 2009, just after completion of yet another enhancement scheme being put into place.

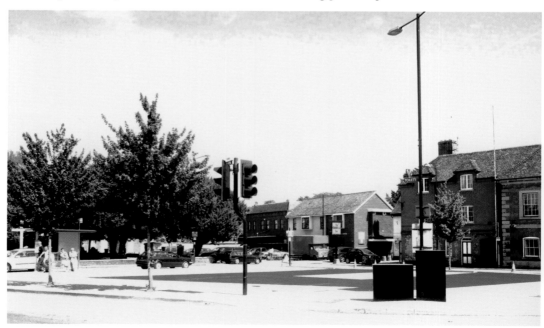

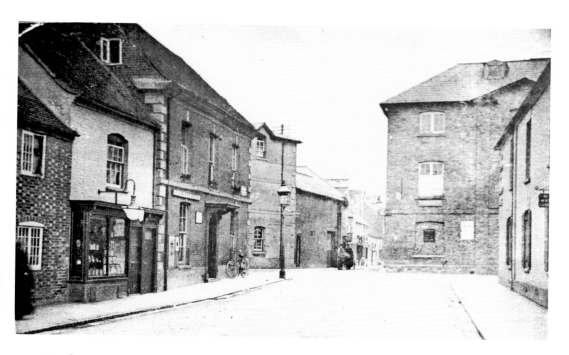

South Street/North Street Junction

The junction from South Street looking across to North Street as it was in the early 1900s. Very little has changed on the left-hand side; on the right, which is now Lloyds Bank, it is very similar today. The imposing building opposite making a narrow entrance to North Street is the old Wool Loft which was demolished soon after the First World War, as it was interfering with the flow of traffic. As you can see, the buildings on the left, apart from changes in paint colouring, have changed very little.

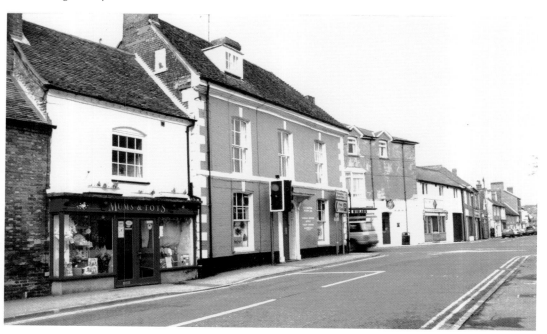

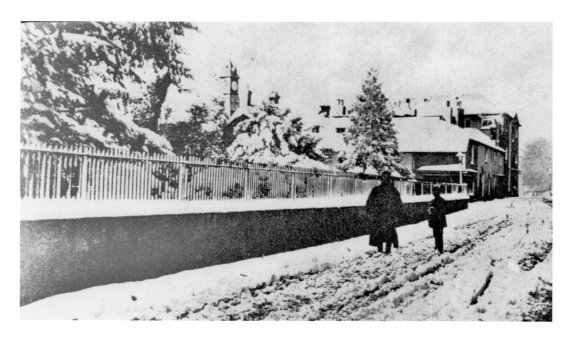

North Street Snow, 1908

This above picture was taken by William Jukes in North Street, looking towards the junction with West Street and South Street in the great snow fall of April 25 1908. The area occupied by the buildings is now the Market Place. These buildings were also demolished along with the Wool Loft just after the First World War. The street between the buildings and St. Mary's Churchyard (shown on left) was known as Brede Street. Church railings have gone, but the buildings to the immediate right, are still *in situ* today.

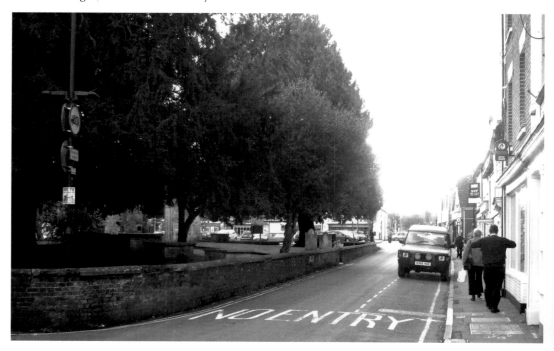

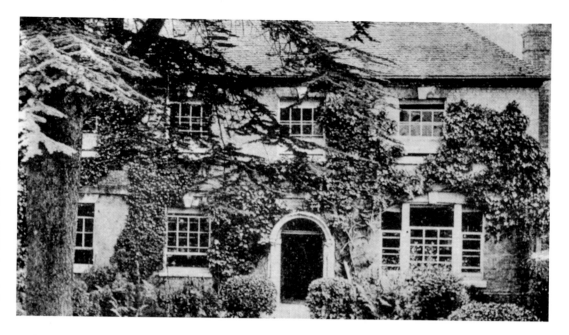

The Wilton Free School

Shown here in the late 1900s, it was founded in 1714 by Walter Dyer who established the school in North Street for the education of twenty poor boys of the parish. They were taught to read and write and grounded in the rules of common arithmetic and the doctrines of the Church of England. After it closed it became a Labour Exchange, later a private house, which it still remains today.

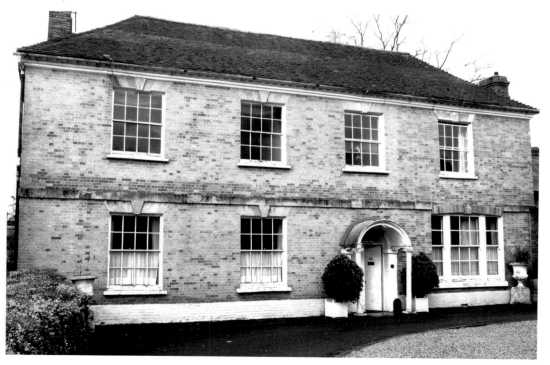

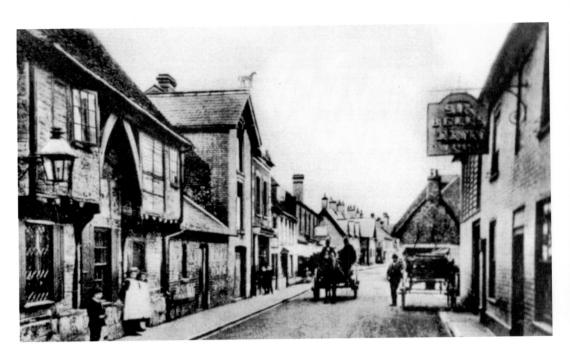

North Street early 1900s

An early 1900s scene in North Street, with the Old House dominating the scene as it still does today. The building with the white horse on the centre of the roof was Thomas Holley's Brewery, today now occupied by the Burnbake Trust. To the right is the Six Bells Inn, which in recent years has changed to an Indian restaurant. The thatched cottage just beyond the inn has also long disappeared.

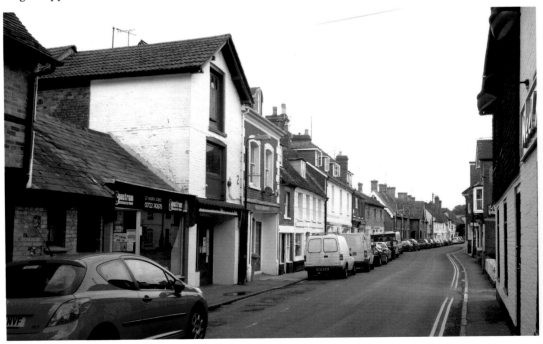

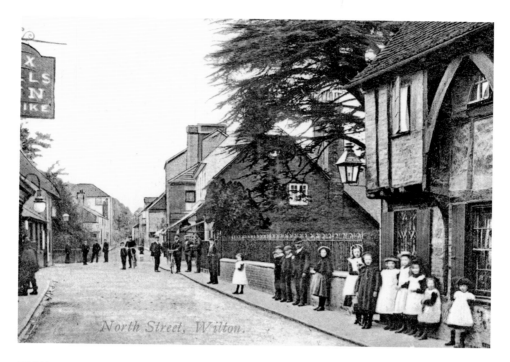

North Street, Wilton.

Old House, 1909

The postmark on the reverse of this postcard is dated 8 August, 1909. Front right is the 'Old House', reputed to be the oldest house in Wilton, and the railings to its left are those of the former Wilton Free School in the picture below taken in the 1990s, the railings have now been replaced by a hedge. The tall buildings at the far end left, just beyond the church wall, have now been demolished and replaced by the Market Place.

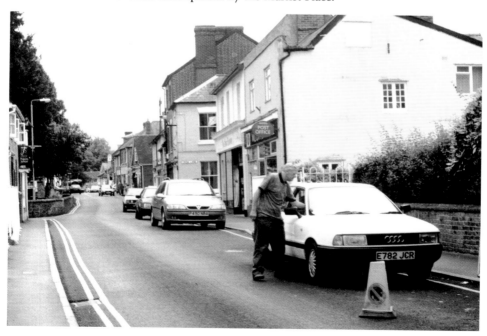

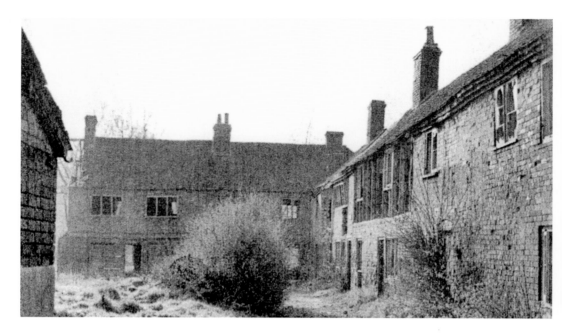

Fancy Row

Photographed just prior to demolition, to make way for more modern council accommodation of flats. The name 'Fancy Row' derives from when the inhabitants of these cottages, during the eighteenth century, worked from home, being employed in making fancy waistcoats, plus elegant linings for gentlemen's dress of the period.

The site became very much run down, being regarded somewhat as a slum, and was demolished in the early 1950s. Today the site is completely transformed. When completed, the area was named 'Churchill Court', in honour of Sir Winston Churchill. The builders were Moulding & Sons. In later years, Wylye Lodge opened, offering its services for sheltered accommodation for the elderly and the handicapped, at the lower end of the site.

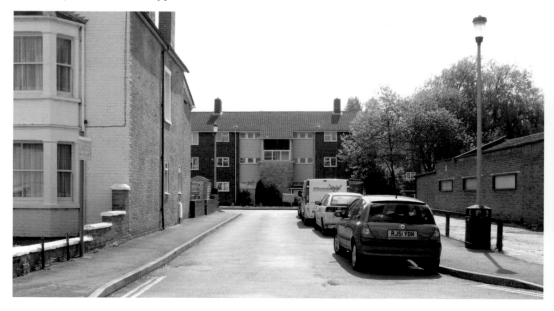

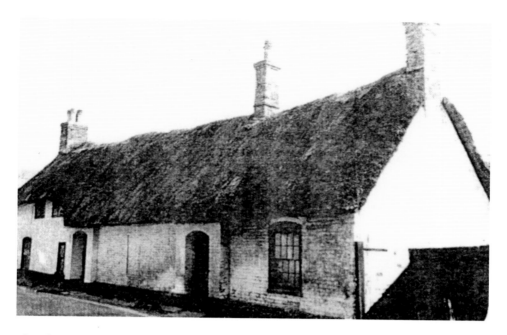

Thatched Building, North Street

This rather forlorn looking thatched building, at the top of North Street, was at one time a private school, run by a very strict disciplinarian. In fact, she was so strict, if she had been born in Dickens's time, she could well have been used as a character in one of his books. Today, the building is a private house. The former schoolroom part was demolished, thus allowing room for the building of a modern dwelling to be built on the adjacent site. The building, between the old school and the house, belongs to the Wilton Carpet Factory, and it actually housed the Town Museum and the Carpet Factory Museum. Unfortunately, costs finally became too much and both closed down at the same time.

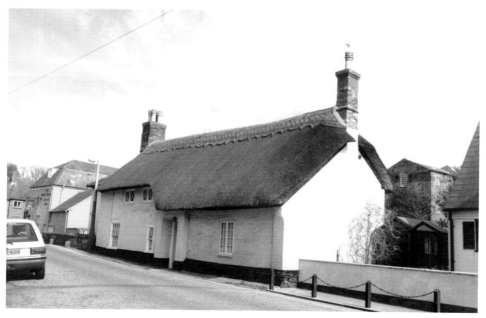

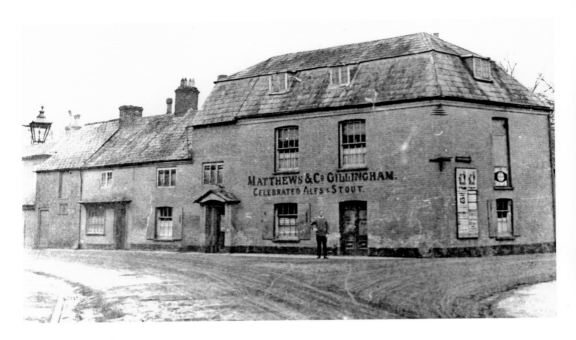

The Wheatsheaf

The Wheatsheaf, at the junction of the Warminster Road and North Street, was locally famous for making its own beer, and was always well patronised by shepherds attending the Sheep Fair at Wilton. One of their traditions held here, many years ago, was an annual custom to determine who would hold the title, 'King of the Shepherds', this being settled in the form of a good fight, with no holds barred. The shop window and doorway to the left of the 'pub', was once a butcher's shop. The modern-day photograph reveals some of the sutle changes, including the level of the road being slightly raised.

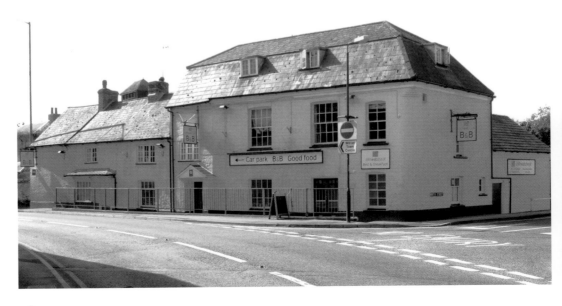

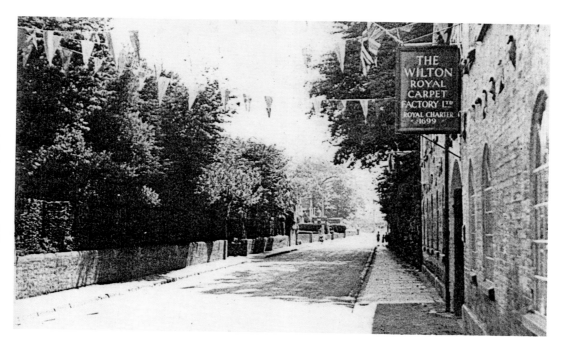

Coronation of Queen Elizabeth II

The flags and bunting stretched across the Warminster Road, from the Carpet Factory, are in place due to celebrations of the Coronation of Queen Elizabeth II, which took place in the town in June 1953. Apart from the decorations, and the removal in more recent times of carpet factory sign, there has been very little change to the street scenery. However, the flow of modern day traffic presents a very different story!

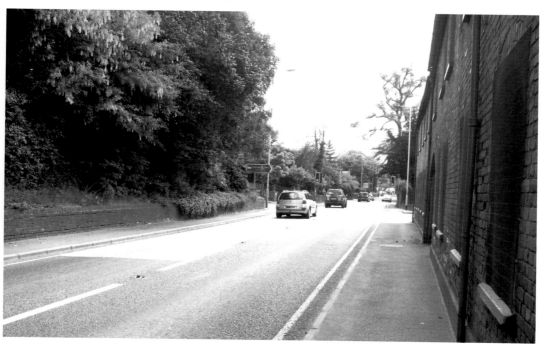

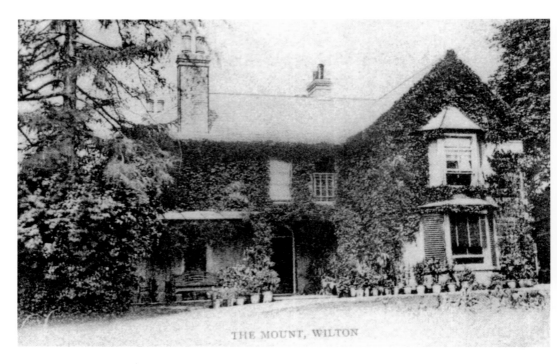

THE MOUNT, WILTON

James Nightingale

In the 1800s this was the home of James Nightingale, a bachelor who lived here with his sister. He was Mayor of the Borough on six occasions, between 1840 and 1872. Also, he was a regular contributor to the *Wiltshire Archaeological Magazine,* writing on many subjects, including articles on the succession of Abbesses of Wilton and notes on Wilton seals. He was also responsible for designing the mayor's chain, which is still in use today. During the late 1900s the house was demolished for building a private housing estate, known as 'Kingsgate'. The Mount was situated approximately where the white house is in the top right of the photograph.

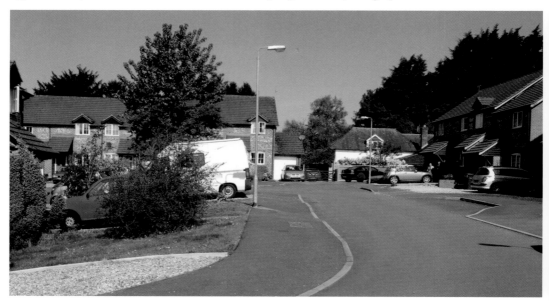

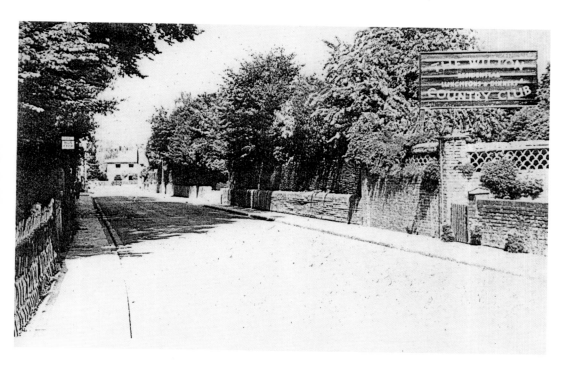

Wilton Country Club

The Wilton Country Club has long gone, and so has the sign. The bus stop is still *in situ*, but today is provided with a shelter. Unfortunately, this along with some other features of street furniture in the town falls prey to attacks of vandalism. The lower photograph was taken early in the day on a Sunday in May spring sunshine, hence a lack of traffic on this usually busy A36 Warminster Road. This scene has changed very little over the years, and if it wasn't for the heavy traffic on weekdays, this could still be a scene from the 1900s.

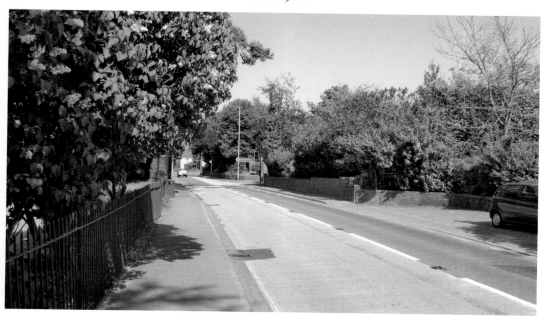

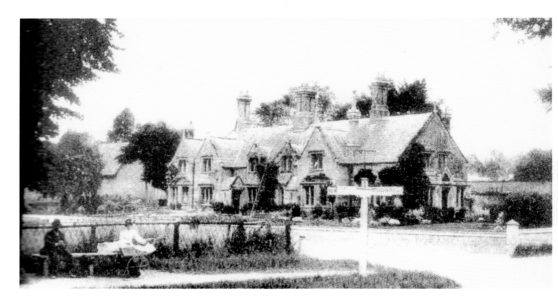

The Cross Roads

A mother with her baby in its pram, alongside with another gentleman, around the second half of the nineteenth century, take a rest on the seat at the Cross Roads. This was a popular place with Wiltonians, who sat here for many decades, watching the world go by. In the background are the Magdalene Trust almshouses. The scene at the crossroads today has completely changed, the road has been widened to make way for the roundabout, installed many years ago, to help speed up the high volume of traffic. The charity of the almshouses is still in existence in these present times.

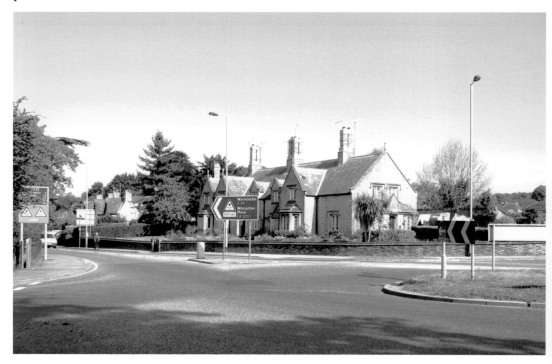

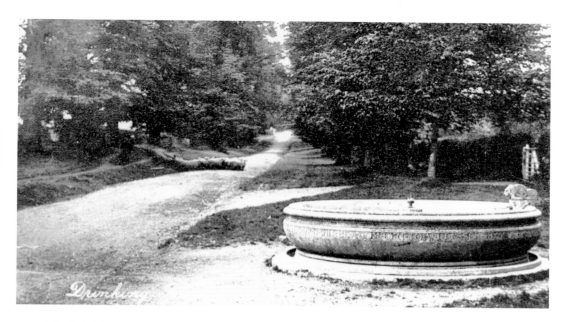

The Drinking Fountain

The drinking fountain at the bottom of the Avenue, was erected in 1901, as a memorial to the late Lord Pembroke, who had died six years earlier. The approach to the Avenue was excavated in the 1840s, a period when many people had fallen on hard times. As a result of this situation, the Pembroke family are thought to have instigated employing many Wiltonians in the making of the road and the planting of trees, to make this new route to into Wilton known then as 'New Cut'. The line across the road is sheep entering what in those days was the lower part of the Sheep Fair Field. As the lower photograph reveals, there have been great changes over the years, with the drinking fountain having been moved to the Recreation Ground, and trees removed on the left to make way for modern day bungalows.

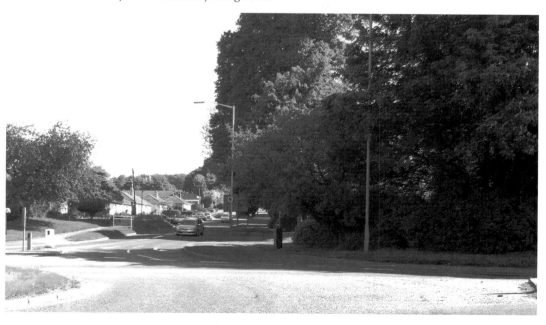

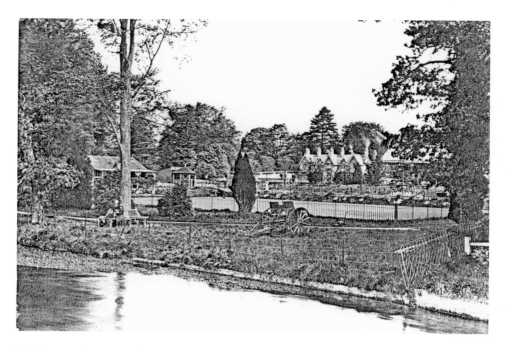

The Recreation Ground

The above photograph of the Recreation Ground, was taken *c.* 1916 during the First World War. Why the mobile field gun is placed there isn't known. However, the bowling green is clearly visible, and the club pavilion can be seen behind the tree to the left. Below, this 2009 photograph shows that there are quite a few changes, the old pavilion was replaced a few years ago with a more modern construction, and visible in the shadows can be seen the drinking fountain that was previously located at the bottom of the Avenue.

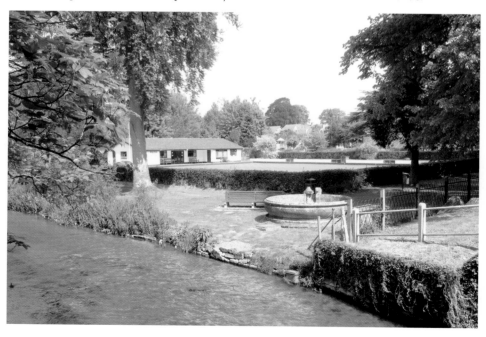

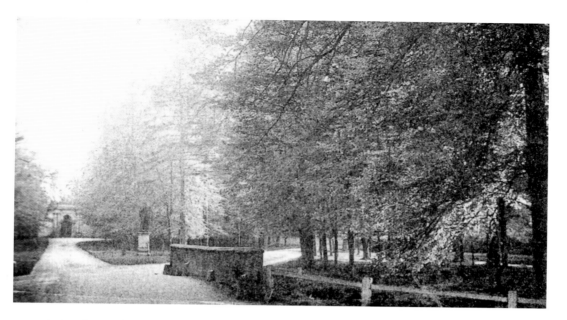

An Unchanged View

As one can see, there is not a lot of change that has taken place since the upper photograph was taken in the early 1900s. Today, there is pavement that has been put *in situ*, as can be seen by the bridge, but what is particularly is noticeable is that the white painted fencing is still in place. On the other side of the bridge, the fencing appears to be the original, with wooden support posts and wooden fencing planks. On this side however, it is wooden fencing posts, but the struts are metal poles, of a more later origin.

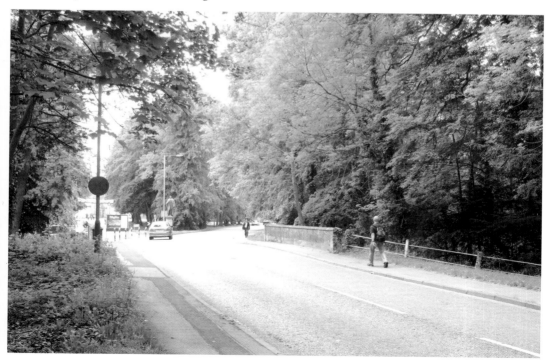

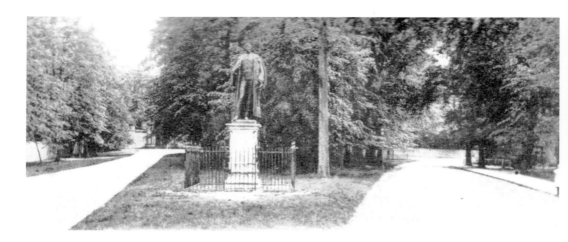

Wilton House

The top picture is an early colour postcard, which was sold by R. Wilkinson & Co., Trowbridge. The message on it is signed by someone with only their initials, W.G.S., but the date is interesting: 9/9/04. It clearly shows to the left, the private roadway leading to the main gate of Wilton House, with the main road into Wilton on the right. The scene is watched over by a statue of the Earl of Pembroke, complete with sword. However, today he no longer has his sword, as it was removed by some American servicemen during the Second World War, the act of removal being witnessed at the time by a young resident of the town.

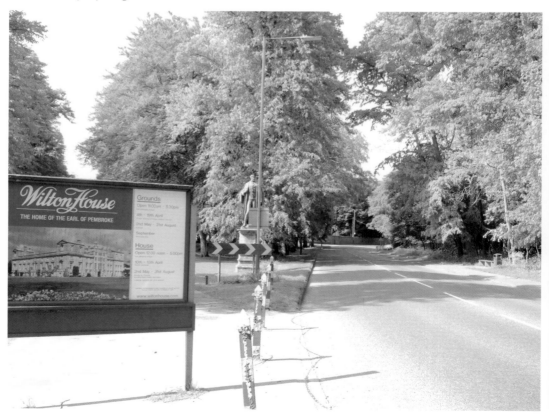

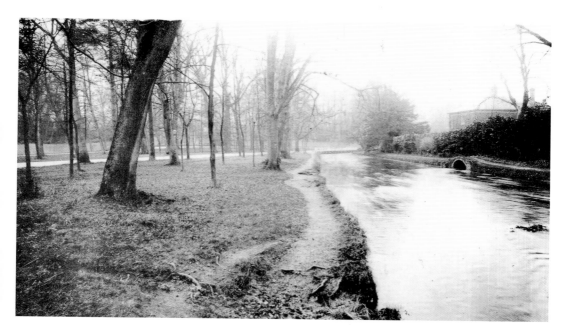

The River, Wilton early 1900s

This location is directly on the opposite side of the road to the pictures on the previous page. It is amazing that all these years later, I was able to find the exact spot where the previous photographer stood to take his shot, to show just how much the scene has changed around a century later. The little bridge on the right is still *in situ*, but can only been seen when directly opposite as, through the years, foliage has taken over. The bank on the right of the path has extended somewhat to support the trees which have grown there over the years. Prior to the bluebells coming on display, there was a lovely display of colour in yellow by a large display of daffodils which were planted here quite a few years ago. This walk by the river is still attracts many people today.

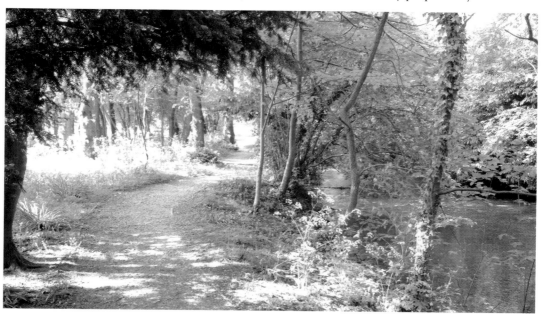

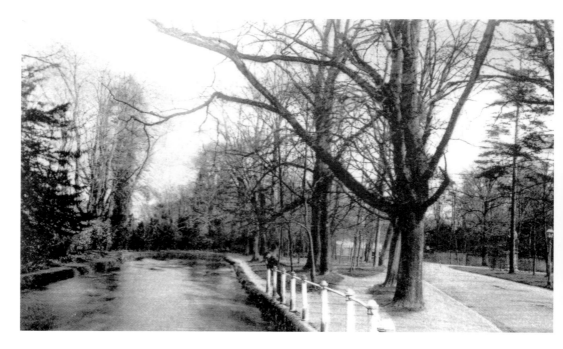

View Opposite Wilton House, 1900s

Above is another view of the area opposite Wilton House, taken early in the 1900s, looking back towards the Recreation Ground and the Cross Roads, revealing just how wide the river was in those times, and how the lack of foliage opens up the scene. It is very different today, although the width of the river is still about the same. Foliage on the trees, however, has really thickened and in the foreground is almost touching the water. Some of the trees in the foreground have been felled, no doubt due to the widening of the road, which is once again to accommodate the heavy flow of traffic in this modern age. The sign with the duck on it is to inform motorists that ducks cross the road at this point to get to the river.

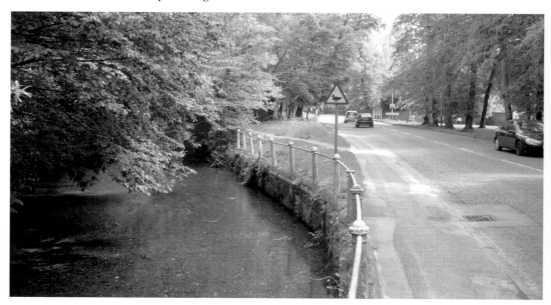

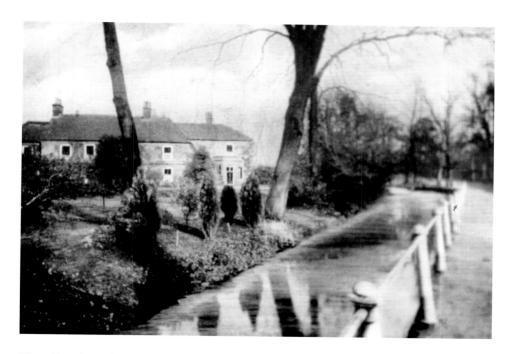

View Showing Island House

This photograph was obviously taken on the same date as the previous one, judging by the view of the trees at the end of the railings. Island House can be clearly seen, and was formerly the home of Col. Crichton Maitland, a former chairman of the local magistrates. Along with his wife, both took an active part in the affairs of the Parish Church and other affairs and events of the town. Their large garden was often the venue for fêtes. Since the picture above was taken, the foliage of the trees has completely obliterated the house and gardens from the road.

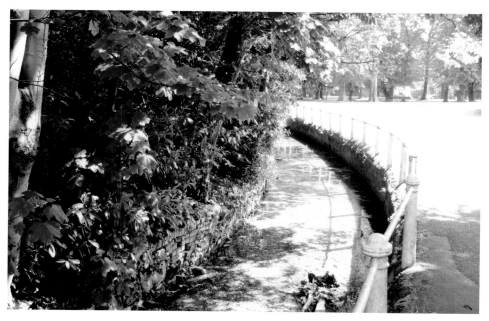

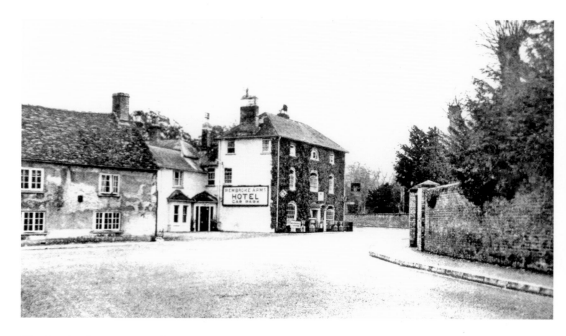

The Pembroke Arms Hotel

This was originally built for visitors to Wilton House, situated directly opposite. Before 1840, the road between the hotel and the roundabout at the junction with the A36, was not in existence. In 1841, the local office of the Customs and Excise were housed in the hotel. In 1870, when the Wiltshire Archaeological Society held a meeting in the town, they partook of a meal here. Since the earlier picture above was taken, the ivy on the walls has been removed, and an extension added for use as a larger restaurant.

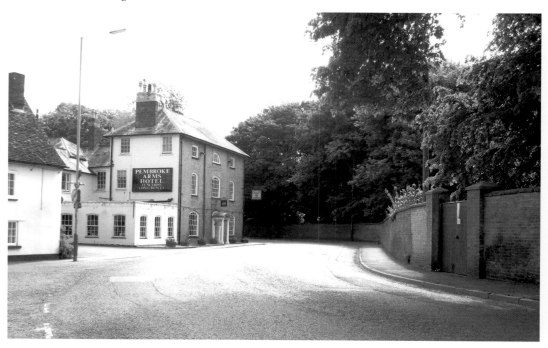

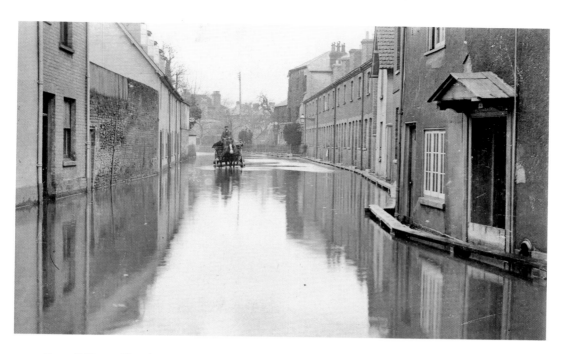

Russell Street Floods, 1915

In 1915, Russell Street was subject to some very serious flooding, as was North Street, at the junction of which allowed the water to enter Russell Street, up to the junction with the main road. It was reported at the time that an eel was seen swimming in the floodwater. The street has hardly altered since the above picture was taken. The only real changes that have taken place are the new houses shown just behind the parked cars, built around the turn of this century.

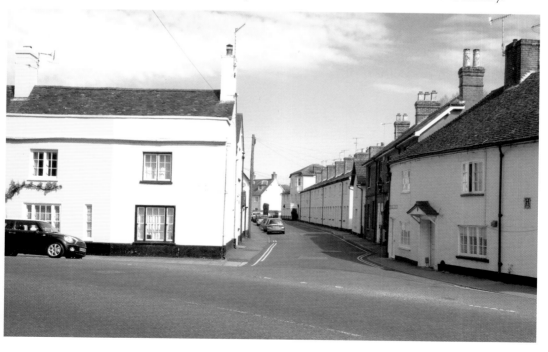

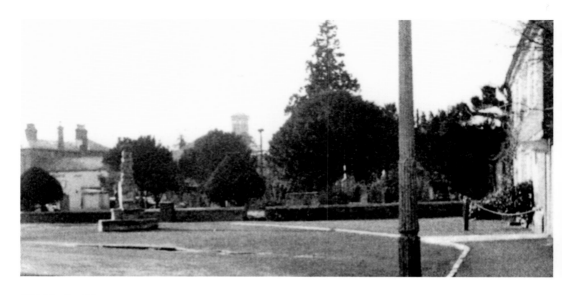

Old Market Place

Shown here with its Market Cross, which in very early times was a guarantee to the public that traders attending markets under this sign, were honest in their dealings. The building on the extreme right is the Old Rectory, of the former parish church of St. Mary. The tower of the present parish church in West Street is clearly visible above the treetops. This is not the case today as there has been a large growth of the trees; now the top of the town's Christmas tree is only just visible. To the left is the building of the Health Centre, which dominates that side of the old market place.

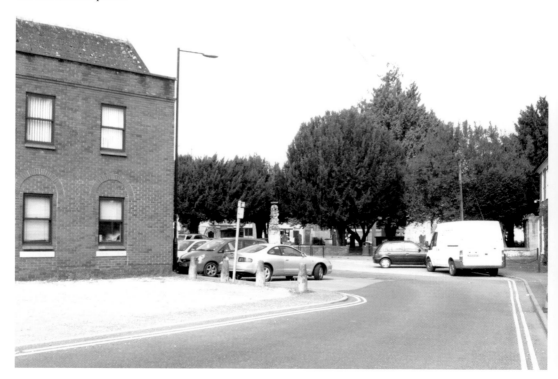

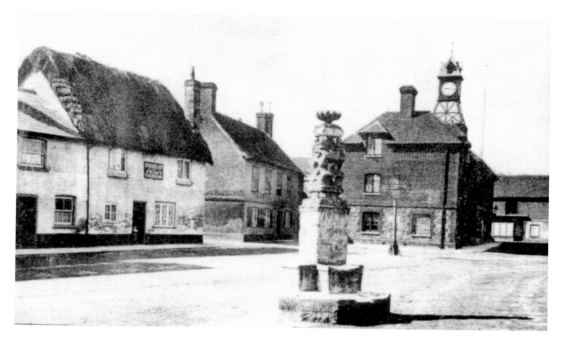

Old Market Place

A view of the Old Market Place, possibly late 1920s to early 1930s. The row of cottages has long gone; the one with the thatch, at this time, was the offices of Whatley's coal merchants. Further along is the Greyhound Inn, to the left of the Market Cross, with the former Town Hall with its clock tower visible on the right.

Today, the Health Centre dominates. The Greyhound is still there, and the Town Hall is now the Baptist Church.

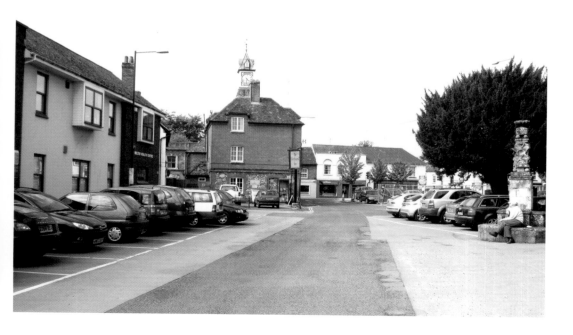

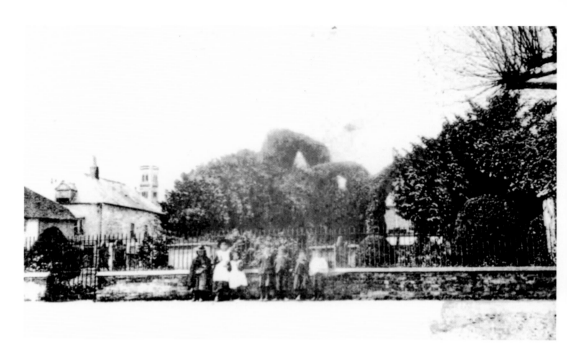

Old Church Wall

Some children stand by the Old Church wall and pose for the photographer, in this classic style idyllic scene of the very early 1900s. The houses to the left were demolished just after the end of the First World War, to make way for the site of the present Market Place. Today the scene is much less tranquil, with it being transformed into modern day use as a cark park.

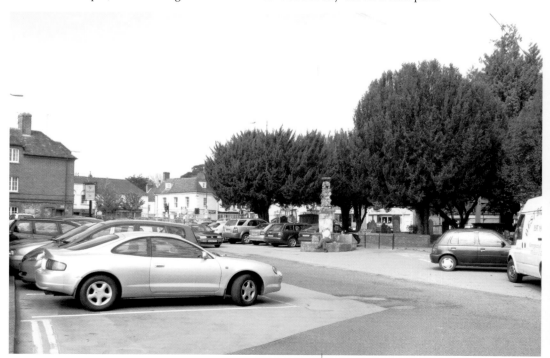

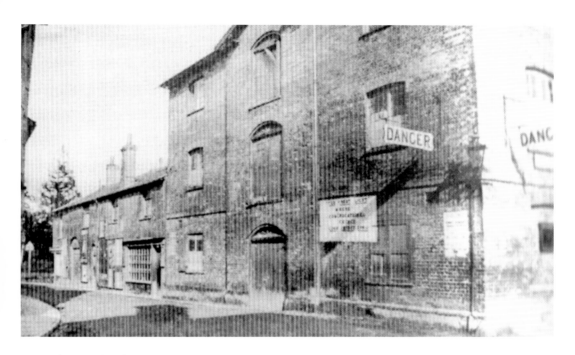

The Wool Loft

This rather imposing building once dominated the centre of the town, was known generally as the Wool Loft. In no way was this an attractive building, but surprisingly there were some very attractive town houses behind it. During the First World War, the building and the houses were taken over by the military for the duration. After the war, the town council decided to demolish the whole area to improve the image of the town and make a new market place, in the centre of which a stone Memorial was erected by public subscription, to Sidney, 14th Earl of Pembroke.

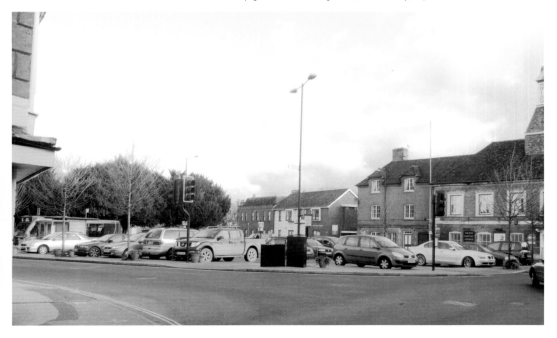

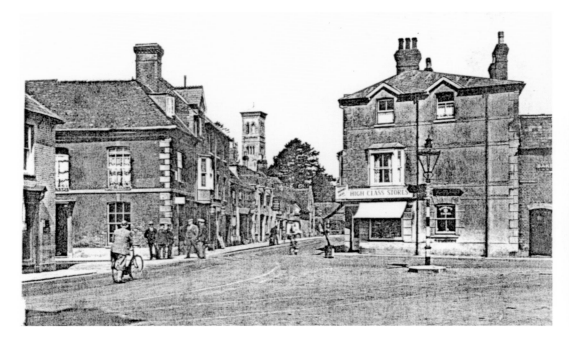

The Market Square

There is plenty of space in the Market Square in this early photograph *c.* late 1920s to early 1930s. At the time, the building, which today is a betting shop, was the post office. Where the now closed HSBC Bank building is today was Redwoods Grocery Store, and where the door is situated just to the right was the store's bakery. Today, this building houses Best Bros, Greengrocers. In the modern photograph below, the tower of the Parish Church is still clearly visible, but replacing the vast amount of space in the foreground shown in the previous picture, is the main car park of the town, photographed just after the enhancement scheme of the Market Place was completed in 2009.

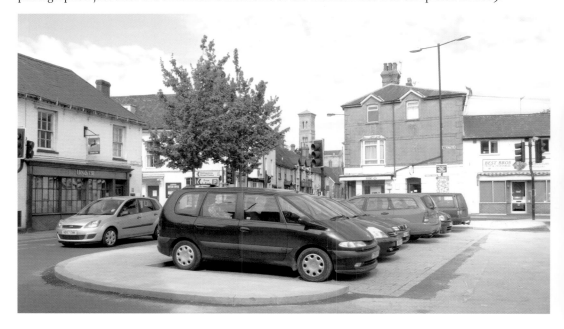

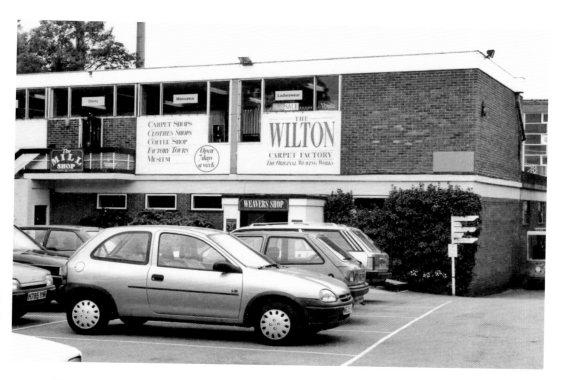

Wilton Shopping Village

The photograph above shows the King Street car park of the Wilton Royal Carpet Factory in 1995, around the time it was decided that the factory site was to be re-utilised as a shopping village, and the factory relocated to a site adjacent to the original factory buildings. The photograph below, taken in May 2009, shows the car park in use as parking for staff and coaches, bringing visitors to the Wilton Shopping Village.

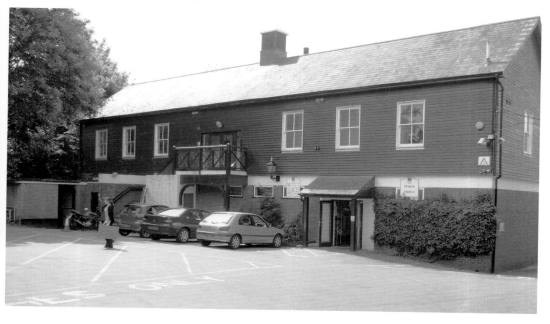

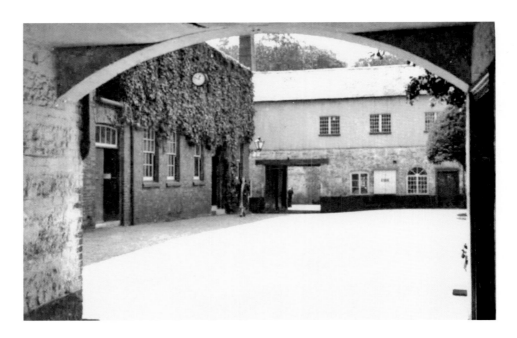

Former Factory Entrance

This photograph taken *c.* 1948/49, was taken just inside the main entrance to the carpet factory, which gave access to the factory directly off King Street. It was through here that all factory workers passed on their way to areas of their work; the weaving sheds, the 'dye house' and the design room and all other sections of the carpet making process. Today, this former factory entrance has been converted into a retail unit in the shopping village, as has the building to the left, and the buildings either side of the archway further down.

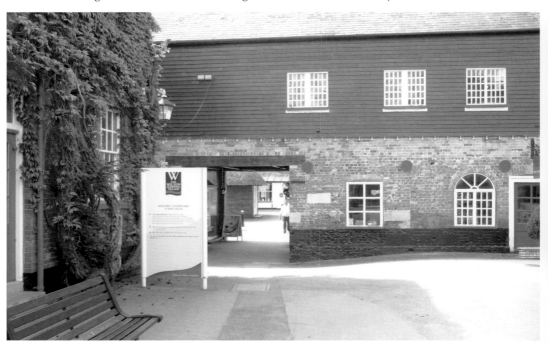

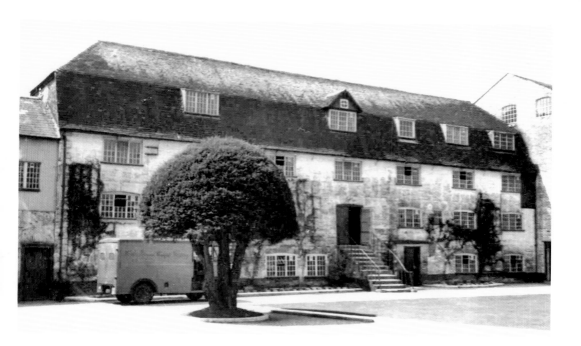

Historic Courtyard

Above is the view across the 'Historic Courtyard', which is the oldest part of the factory. As can be seen in the picture below, there has been very little change with the building, or indeed the general view. A tower type of building on the right hand side was added, containing a lift, to help move goods around the floors. Until a few years ago, one floor level contained a Carpet Factory and a Wilton Museum, both of which are now unfortunately no longer there, despite their popularity with tourists in earlier times.

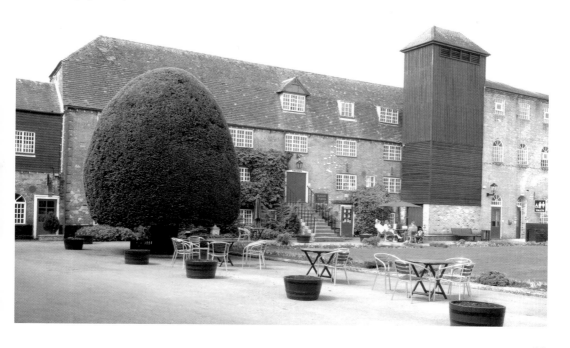

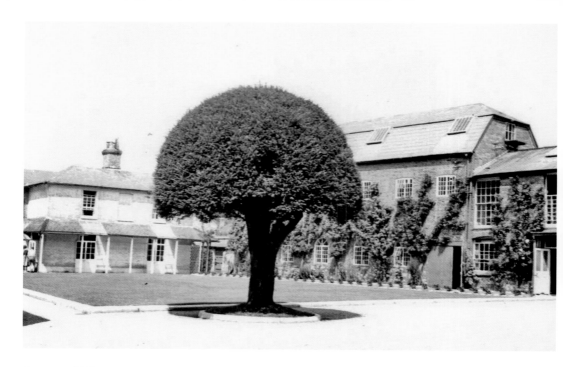

Courtyard View

Here is the opposite side to the previous photographs, also taken *c.* 1948/49, showing some of the buildings used for offices. The house at the far end of the grass section, at the time, was the factory manager's house and it was the first house in Wilton to have electricity. When it was being refitted to be converted into tearooms during 2008, some of the original electrical fittings were still *in situ*, although obviously not in use.

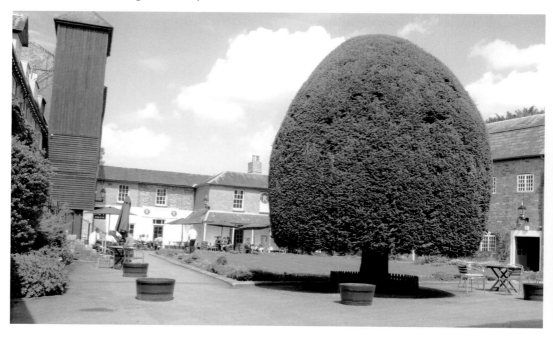

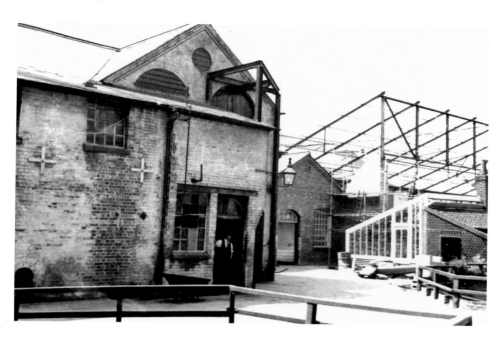

The Wilton Shed

In the adjacent courtyard, the building on the left is the old stoke house, possibly used as the central point to pump heating into the factory buildings. The buildings to the right were the weaving sheds, one of which was known as the 'Wilton Shed', where the famous Wilton Weave carpets were produced, which were sold all over the world. The Royal Family were also customers, and this enabled the factory to be known as the 'Wilton Royal Carpet Factory', until it was taken over by an American firm, 'Carpets International' in the 1990s, which caused shock waves throughout the town. The weaving sheds were converted into a retail shop for the Edinburgh Woollen Mill.

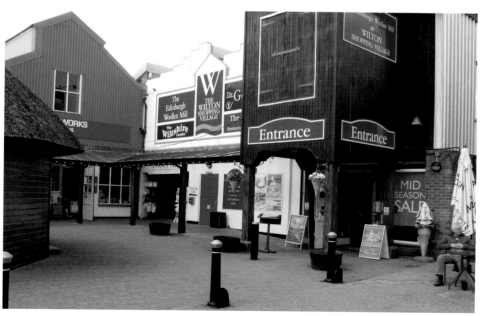

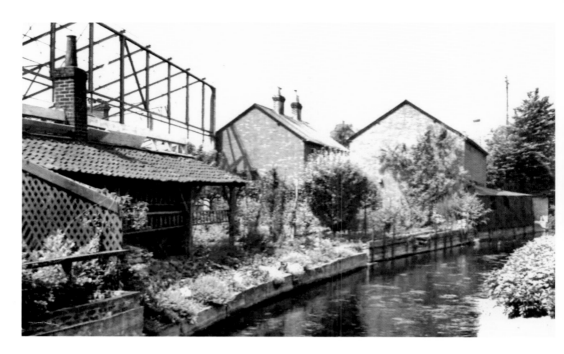

The River Wylye

Above is the view taken in the post war period of 1948/49, showing what appears to be new weaving sheds under construction. The River Wylye ambles slowly through the factory on what appears to be a lovely sunny summer's day, reflecting the buildings as it passes through. Today the Edinburgh Woollen Mill occupies the site, and the covered walkway in the picture below allows the factory workers a direct access to the factory buildings, now situated in a complex on the south-western side of the site.

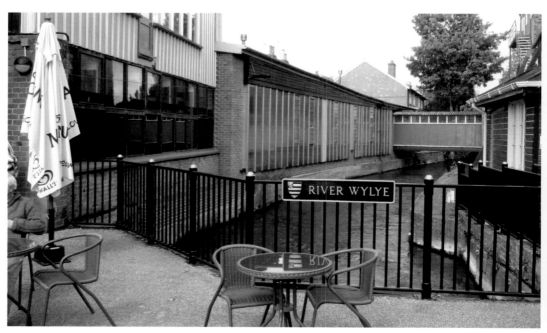

RIVER WYLYE

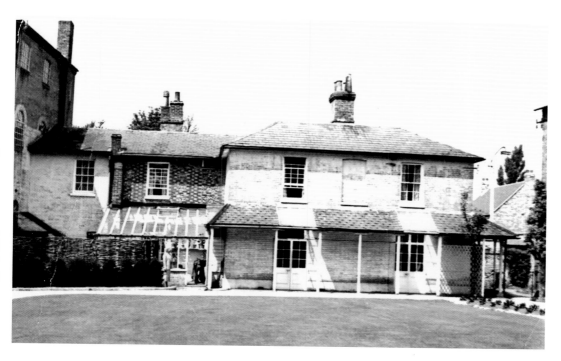

The Factory Manager's House

Above is the factory manager's house, at the time when Mr. Aston was the manager. The area of grass was often used to show off the larger carpets that were made at the factory, especially in periods before the Second World War. Today the house is now the Polly Tea Room, but prior to that it was a retail gift-shop outlet known as 'Old Traditions'. Because the building is listed, there were some problems in its change of use.

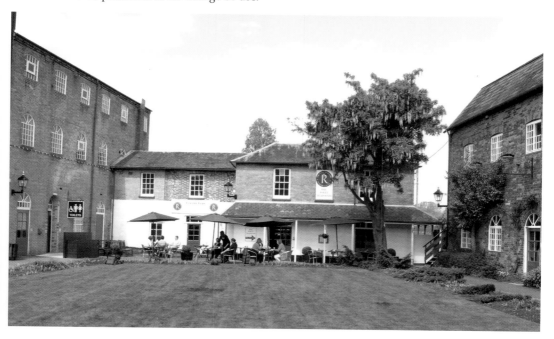

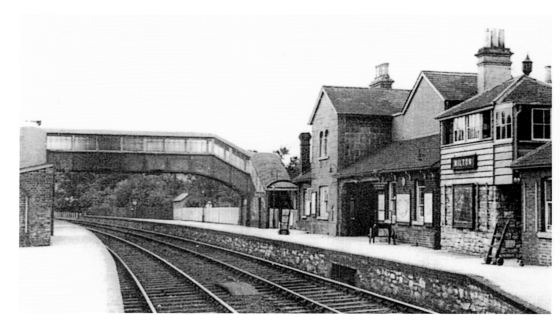

The Railway Station

The railway played a very important part in the economy of the town, not only with passenger traffic; it also had a flourishing goods trade. Many despatches of Wilton Carpets started their journey from here to various destinations all over the country. The station was also well known for despatching thousands of lettuces during the summer season. There was also a siding to the rear of the down platform, which on the days Sheep Fairs were held, was in constant use discharging sheep at the special loading dock, which allowed direct access to the actual field. This siding was situated approximately where the fence is today, shown below.

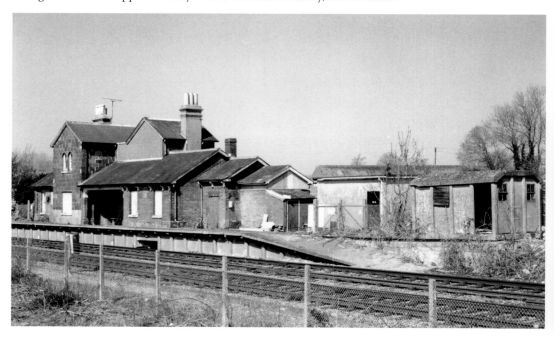

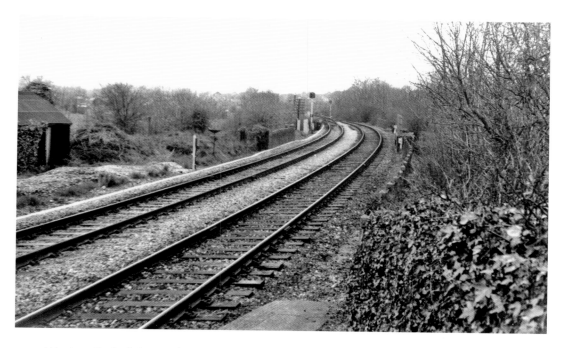

Western End of the Station

Above the line at the western end of the station as it was on 10/04/1982, looking down the main line towards Exeter. Just after the bend, this line converts to a single line working in different sections to Exeter. The old platelayer's hut is just visible on the left hand side. The modern view was taken twenty-three years later, and it reveals how the vegetation has grown in that time, completely swamping the former platform. Also it can be seen that the platelayer's hut has since been demolished and fencing has been installed.

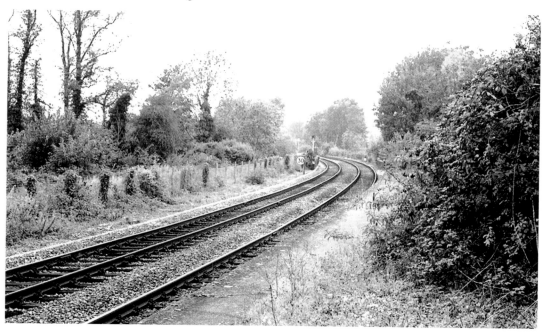

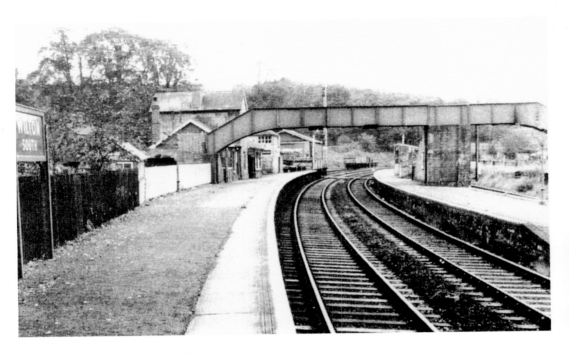

Wilton South and Wilton North

In the days just after British Rail took over the running of the railway, the station was renamed, 'Wilton South', as the former GWR station was also named 'Wilton'. To avoid further confusion, that station was named 'Wilton North'. The photograph above shows the station around the mid-1950s, with the weatherproof covering having been removed from the footbridge. Below is the station in October 2005.

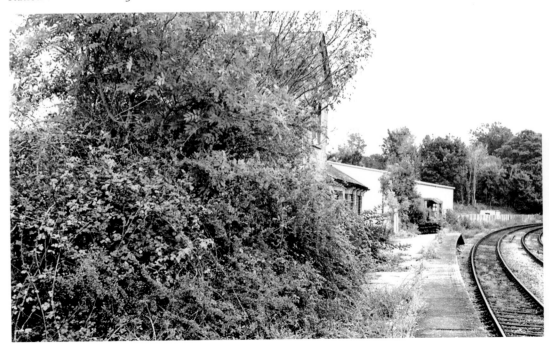

Shunting Duties at Wilton South

Here is a Drummond T9 on shunting duties at Wilton South, just about to enter the siding on the up-line side, to pick up some trucks. The picture on the right could well have been taken late on a Saturday afternoon, as on these afternoons around 4 p.m., extensive shunting operations used to take place. All these photographs were taken from the Avenue Bridge, which runs over the line at the Salisbury end of the station. Below is the same scene today, the sidings long gone, and new industrial buildings built on the site of the former sidings and station yard.

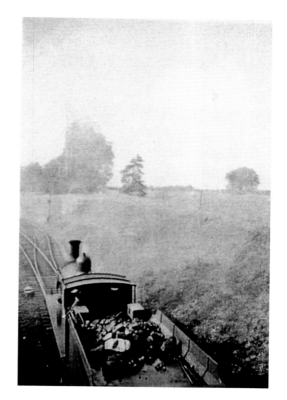

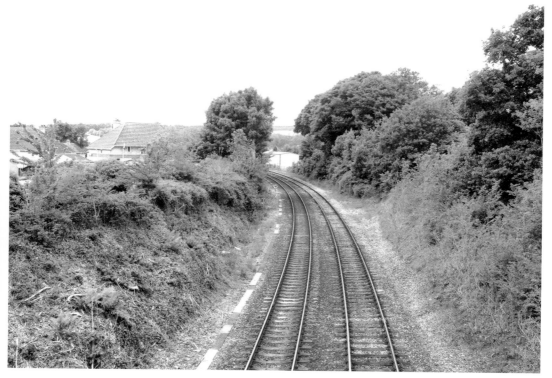

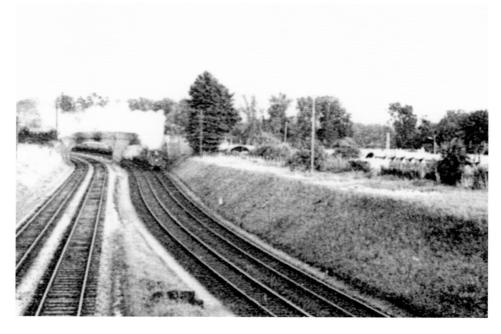

Avenue Bridge Views

These two photographs are taken from the opposite side of the Avenue Bridge, looking towards Salisbury. On the left is the former GWR main line to Bristol and Cardiff, and on the right, to Exeter and West Country. Above is shown a Waterloo to Exeter express about to pass under the Avenue Bridge and Wilton South Station. This picture was taken in the late 1940s, showing military huts of the Army at Southern Command, their HQ at this time being situated up the Avenue. Below is a view taken in May 2009.

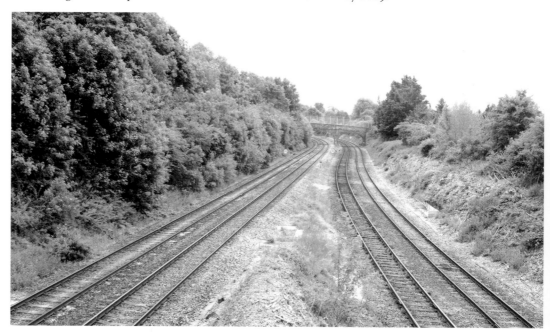

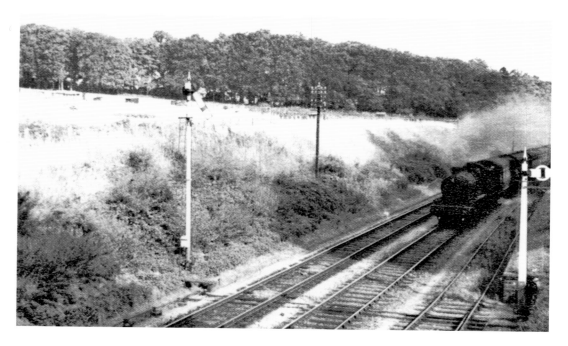

Kingsway Bridge

Photographed in 1949 from the Kingsway Bridge, which passes over the former GWR main line, is a Bristol and Cardiff express. Just visible on the right is a siding which allowed animals to be off loaded, then brought up the slope on to lorries to be taken to local farms. The location of the signal was to allow the driver easier visibility, due to slight curvature of the line. Below is the same view photographed in May 2009, with the old loading platform in an overgrown state to the right.

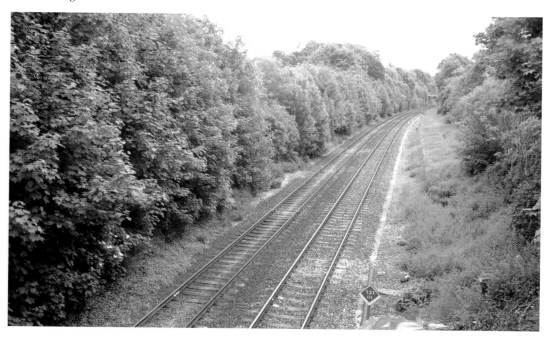

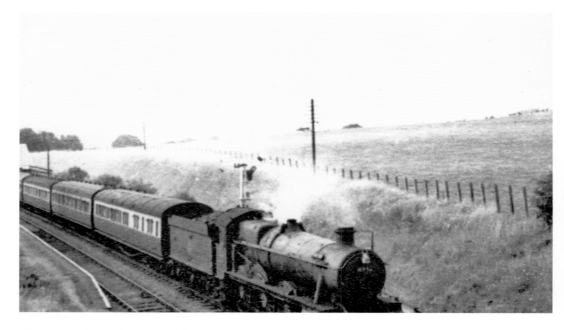

Kingsway Bridge, Opposite Side

The above photograph, taken in 1949, shows a Cardiff to Salisbury express passing through the GWR station from the Kingsway Bridge on the opposite side. The down platform to Bristol is just visible on the left. On the other side of the train is a siding, which passed immediately behind the up platform. The two stations were not very far apart as the crow flies, and one could walk between them in around seven to ten minutes. In the heyday of privatisation, the stations were very keen competitors, each with their Station Masters trying to out do each other with both passenger and goods trade. With nationalisation, much of this rivalry ceased. In May 2009, shown below, the picturesque scene across the fields is now completely obliterated by the trees that have firmly established themselves on the embankments.

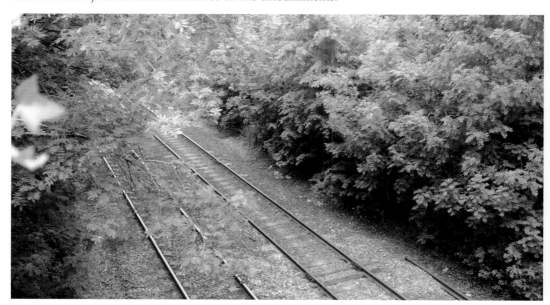

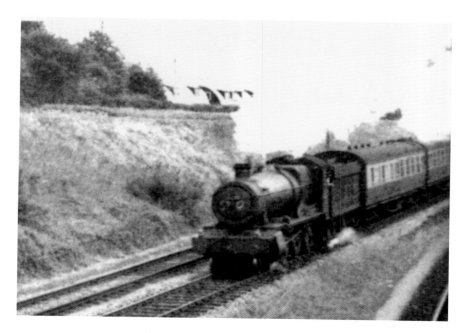

Avenue Bridge

Above, this time a Salisbury to Cardiff express, is running adjacent to the Salisbury to Exeter route, on the Salisbury side of the Avenue Bridge, *c.* 1948/49. Once again there is the presence of the army at Southern Command, with the nissen huts clearly visible. Originally these two ran by their own separate routes into Salisbury, but in more recent times, the former GWR line was merged into the Southern route at Quidhampton Junction. Below is the scene photographed in May 2009.

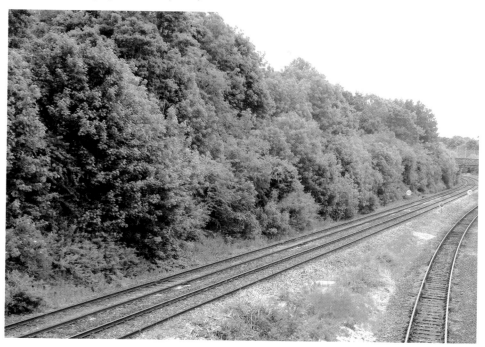

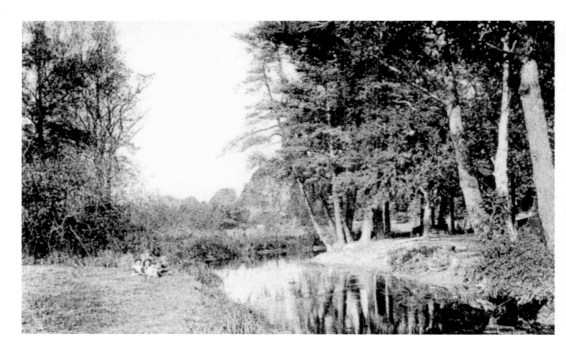

Castle Meadow

We know that the above picture was taken in Castle Meadow, as the LSWR Railway bridge is just visible in the centre background. The picture was taken in the early 1900s, as since then many changes have been made to the water and river courses, including the one shown above. In the late 1940s the council purchased the meadow as a playing field, and raised the level of the ground by several feet to avoid flooding, obliterating all traces of former river courses. I used some old Ordnance Survey maps to locate the area where the children posed, which were certainly revealing in showing how many changes had been made to watercourses and the river.

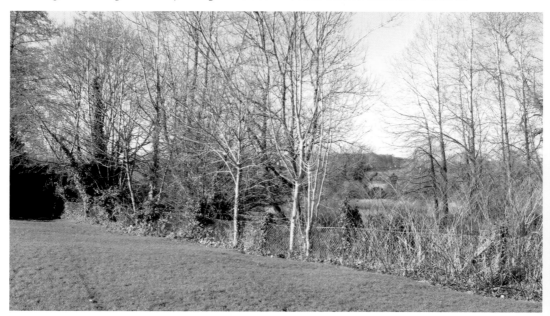

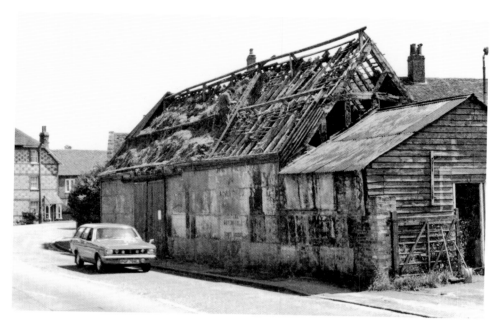

Whatley's the Coal Merchants

Above is the old barn, which stood at the bottom of the Shaftesbury Road, opposite the Bell Inn. This picture was taken soon after demolition commenced in the late 1980s. A feature of the barn was that its outer walls were covered in large advertisements, which included some for the cinemas in Salisbury. The smaller building attached to it was the yard office. After it had been cleared, the site was used for sheltered housing for the elderly. The housing development is named St. John's Priory, which is the name of the small church further down the round, actually built on the corner. This church was illustrated at the beginning of the book.

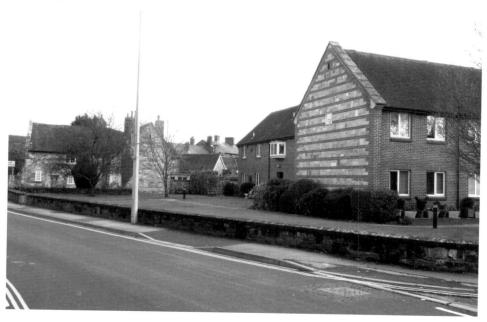

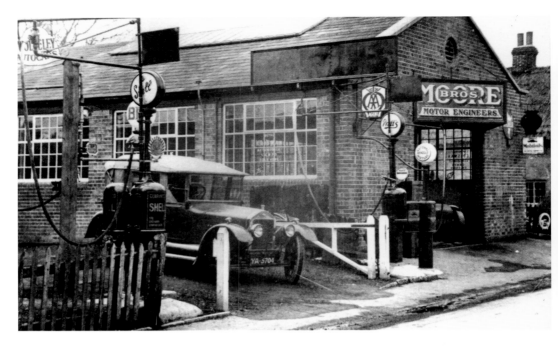

Engineering Workshop in Shaftesbury Road

This business was started by Henry and William Moore, two brothers, not long after the ending of the First World War. Many of the repairs they carried out were not only to many types of vehicles, but a majority were also carried out on Wolsey cars, as the brothers were actually agents for that well-known company. They also sold petrol and did a roaring trade during the Second World War, especially with American soldiers. In later years they manufactured pistons, but eventually modern houses were built on the site.

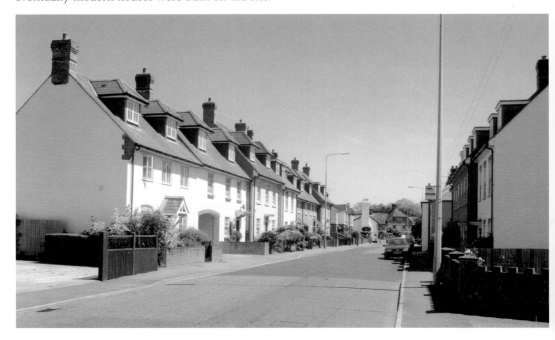

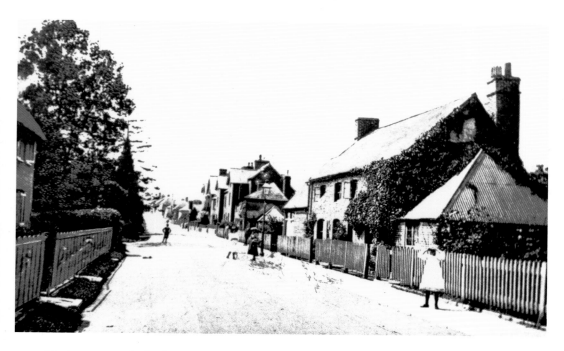

Ditchampton, Shaftesbury Road
In earlier years, this part of the Shaftesbury Road was more commonly known as Ditchampton. The name derived from all the drainage ditches that were dug in a wide area of this part of the town, to help eleviate flooding. Today this road forms part of the A30, all the way down to the West Country, which in summertime is exceptionally busy. Children would definitely not be able to stand in those positions these days.

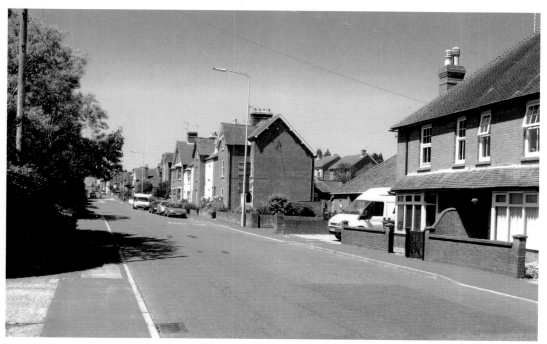

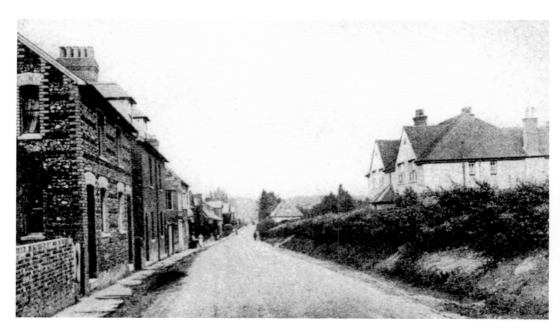

Top of Shaftesbury Road

From near the top of Shaftesbury Road, looking down into the town, there have been more changes over the years. The banking has totally disappeared, and the two houses on the right appear to still be *in situ*, despite some cosmetic alterations. What seems to be amazing, with the exception of the modern car in the foreground, is that on the left, there appears to be very little visible change to this area of the town.

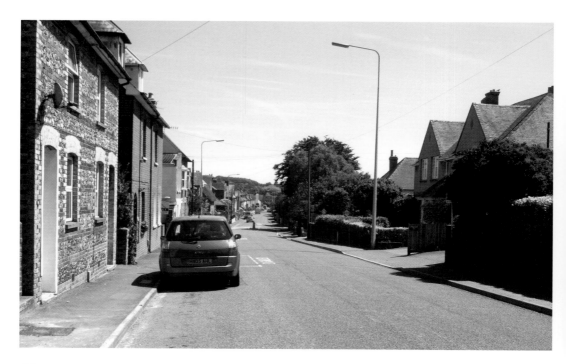

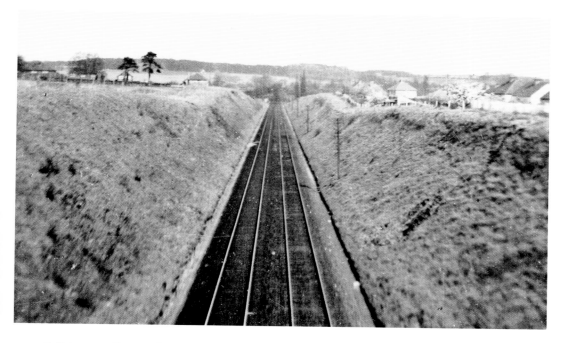

Salisbury to Exeter Line

The photograph above was taken by myself in 1955, and shows the Salisbury to Exeter main line, looking towards Wilton South Station. In those days there was double track, the high embankments were well cut back and tidy with lush green grass. In June 2009, it's completely different, as the line has been singled for many years, and trees have taken over the embankments. What a difference fifty-four years have made.

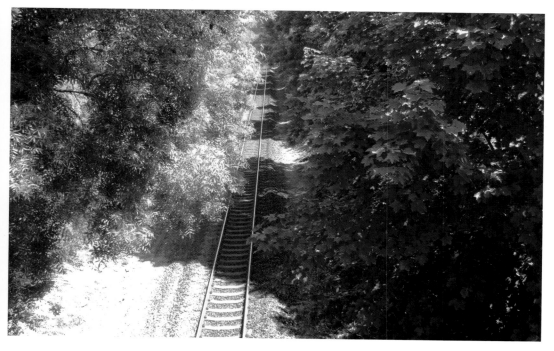

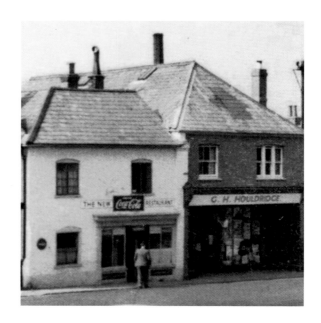

Market Place, 1950s

This scene is very reminiscent of life in the town. The café at that time was called 'The New Restaurant'; it sold Coca Cola and also had a juke box. The drapery shop next door belonged to Miss Houldridge, and concentrated on knitting wools and sewing items. When the business closed it did become a small supermarket, owned by a Mr. Frowd. Today the shop has been completely transformed, and is now Lloyds Pharmacy. The café is still there at the time of writing, having been refurbished and taken over by new owners in May 2009.

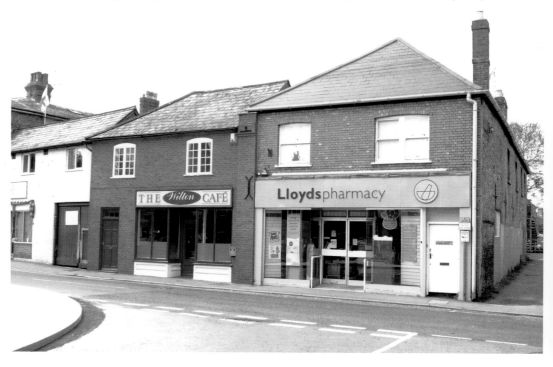

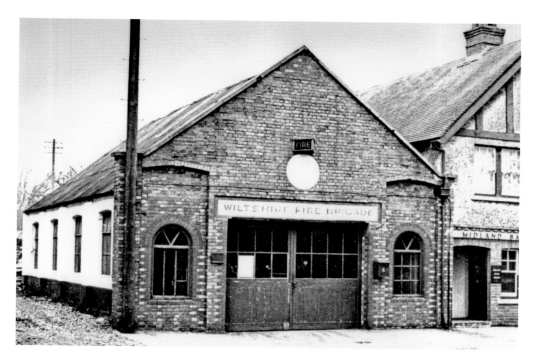

Wilton Fire Station

For many years the Wilton Fire Station was a familiar sight on this location, with the Midland Bank as its neighbour. It was only a sub-station and was manned by a volunteer crew, who were often called out from their employment to put out a fire, or attend at a road accident. In later years a new station was built near the Recreation Ground. The old fire station was converted in a hardware store, and during the 1990s it became a convenience store.

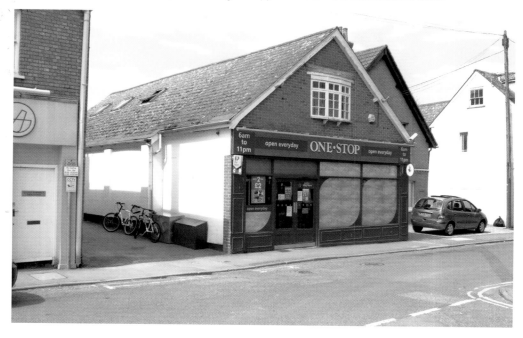

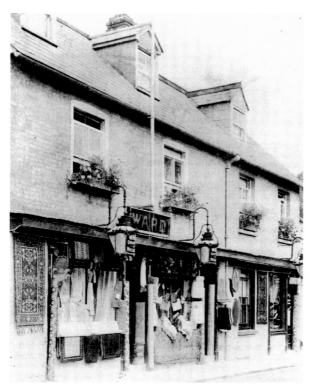

Joseph Ward

The 1871 census shows that Joseph Ward is a linen draper, living above the shop in North Street. He had two daughters, Mary and Jane, who he employed as assistants in his shop. In later years the first section became the Greydawn Café, then became a branch of Barclays Bank, which closed about 2005. Since then it has remained derelict, but builders have now moved in so it is now a case of wait and see. The shop next door is a hairdressers.

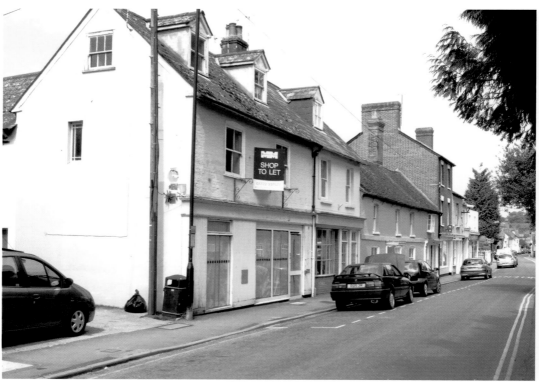

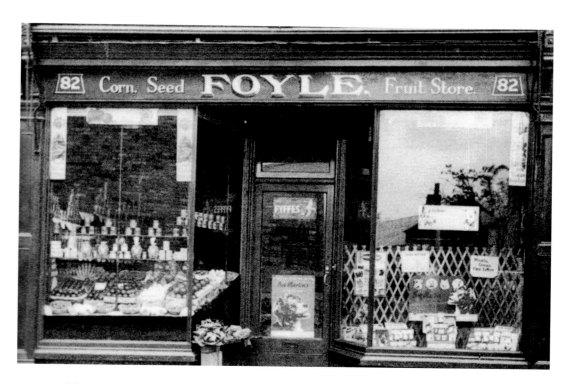

Foyle's Corn and Seed Shop

Situated on North Street, this was a well established and successful business. The photograph above is believed to have been taken around 1935. It was noted for its fruit and good quality seeds. It kept going through the Second World War and remained in business until the late 1950s. It then became an antique shop, which survived during two different ownerships, and then it became a ladies' hairdresser. During the years, except for differing colours of paint and a change of numbering, the look of the frontage has not changed through the years.

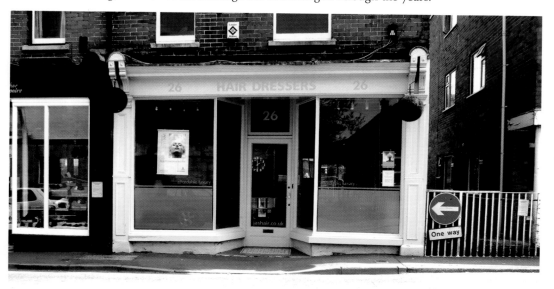

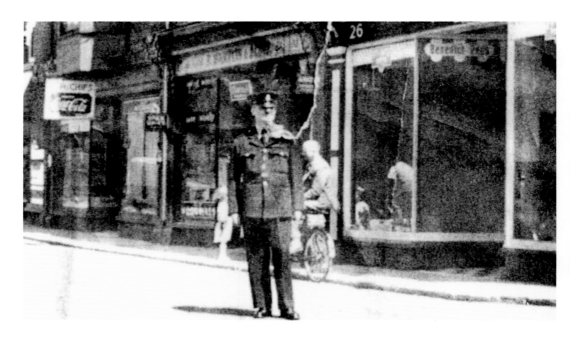

PC Nicholas, North Street

Pictured above, PC Nicholas, one of the town's policemen, is seen standing in North Street, keeping law and order. He was one of the policemen of the town, who in those days were based in the police station in the Wilton Road; today, the site has been turned into a private housing estate. Immediately behind him is 'Barton's Food Store'. Today, it is Coombs shoe shop, which it has been now for many years. Next door, to the left, is the fish and chip shop, where in my youth one could get a bag of freshly cooked chips for the princely sum of *6d* (two and a half pence).

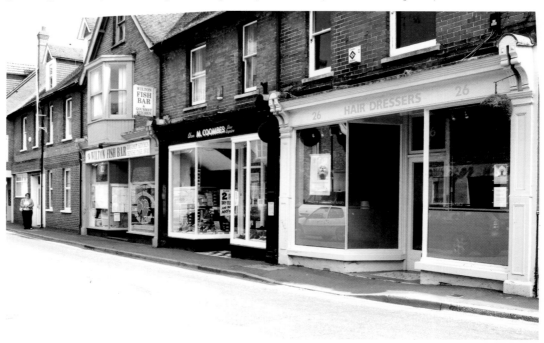

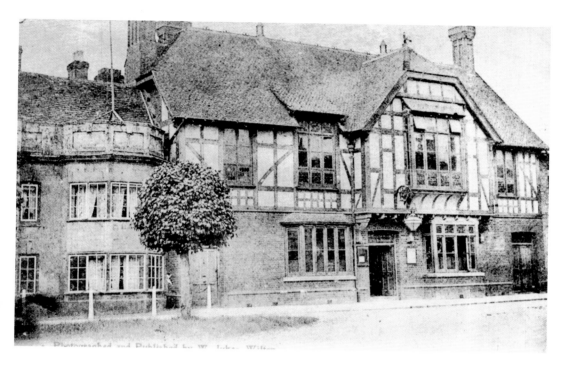

Talbot & Wyvern Hall

At the western end of Kingsbury Square stood this rather impressive building known as the Talbot and Wyvern Hall, which became better known in later years locally as the Coffee Tavern. Its foundation stone was laid in 1873 by Sir Edmund Antrobus, MP for Wilton. It was the headquarters of the Wilton Total Abstinence Society. At the time one-sixth of the town's population were teetotal, so it became a popular venue for all ages. Many events were held here over the years, and during the First World War many fund raising events were held in aid of the war effort.

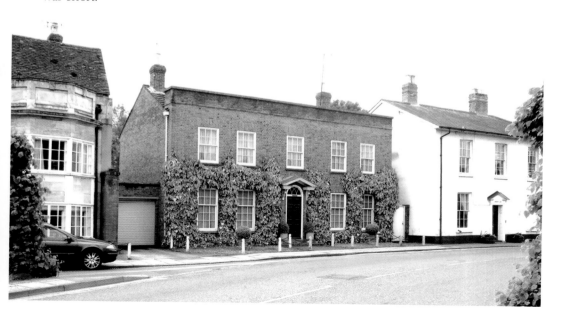

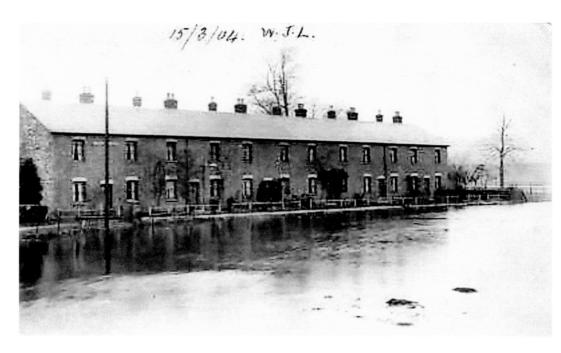

15/3/04. W. J. L.

Wiley Terrace, North Street

The above photograph was taken by my grandfather, William James Lane, from the bridge that runs over the River Wylye in North Street. Fortunately, he actually dated the photograph on the day it was taken. At the time he was employed as a weaver in the carpet factory, but was also a part-time Wilton correspondent for the *Salisbury Journal*. When he was engaged on this work, he quite often took photographs, which appeared with his reports. This area, like many others in Wilton, was prone to heavy flooding in those times.

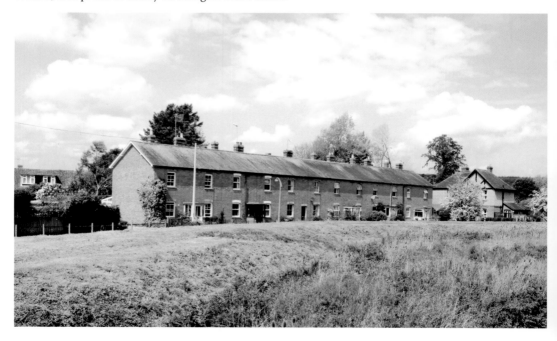

Pound Meadow

At the top end of North Street in the 1950s; on the left you can see the gates to Pound Meadow. This is next to the pound where in earlier times stray animals were held until they were claimed. Naturally the meadow was used for much larger animals, such as sheep or cows. During earlier times at the Wilton Sheep Fair, sheep would be kept overnight. In more recent times the meadow has been transformed into an area for preservation of wildlife and plants. The row of houses just over the bridge were originally built for workers at the carpet factory. In the centre of the row was a special room, in which meetings were held of the Weavers Guild.

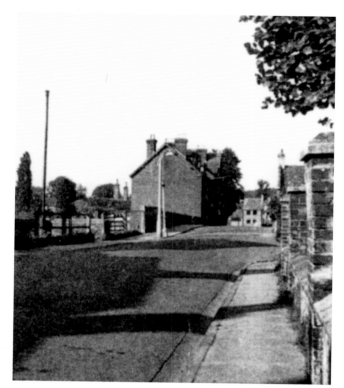

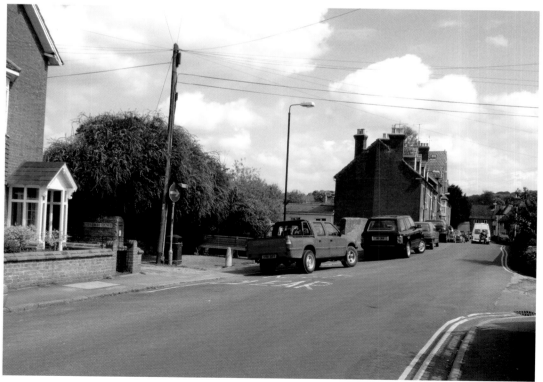

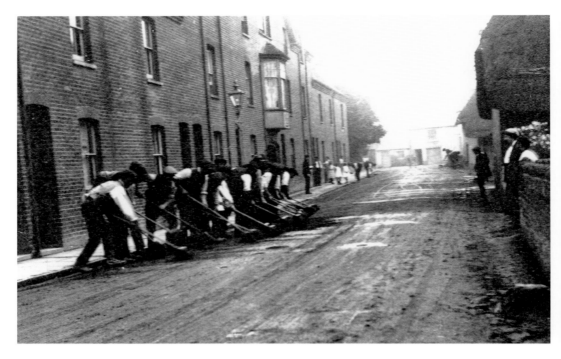

Road Repairs

In this picture taken by my grandfather, workmen are seen attending to the surface of the road, which by the look of it, seems to still be surfaced with dirt. Apart from a modern road surface, and cars parked in front of the houses, very little seems to have changed. In both photographs, the room in which meetings of the Weavers Guild were held, is easily established by the prominence of the bay window, which is clearly visible.

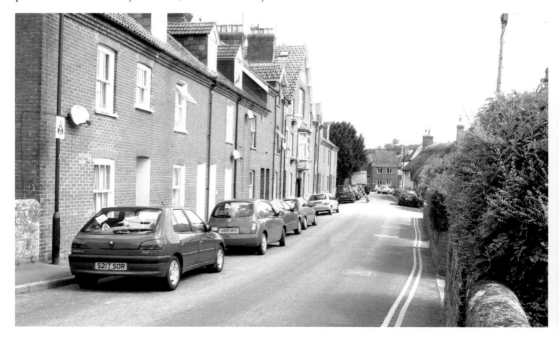

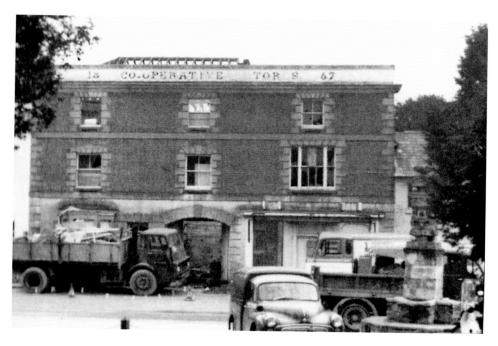

Wilton Carpet Factory

Built on the site of the original Wilton Carpet Factory, the Wilton and District Co-op stores were erected in 1867, serving Wiltonians and people from many surrounding villages, for just over one hundred years. In around 1978, demolition commenced which also included two cottages to the right, making way for another development, the Wilton Health Centre, which opened in 1979. An old map of the area, when the carpet factory was on the site, shows the road on the left, leading to Kingsbury Square, being named as 'Carpet Walk'.

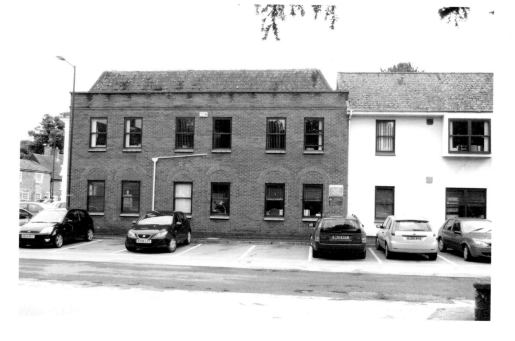

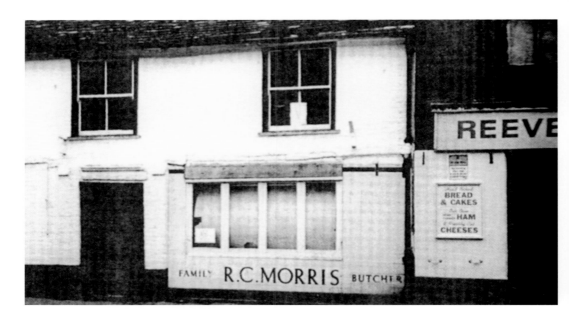

Morris the Butcher

Although Morris the family butcher's shop in West Street was rather small, it served many customers. This was a well-known family business in West Street for quite a time, which unfortunately fell victim, along with many others, to the arrival of the large supermarket chains. Eventually, the shop itself was demolished, to make way for a passage to lead through to a gardening shop, which also acted as a pedestrian route through to North Street, avoiding the dangerous corner by the former HSBC Bank building.

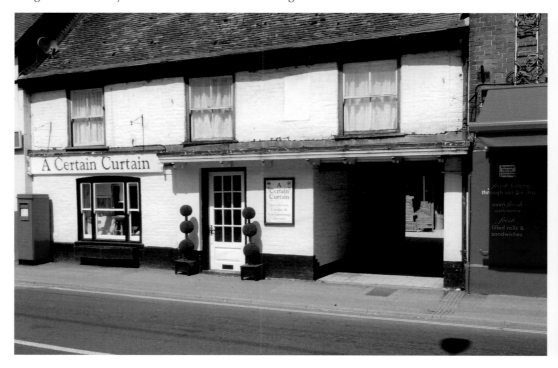

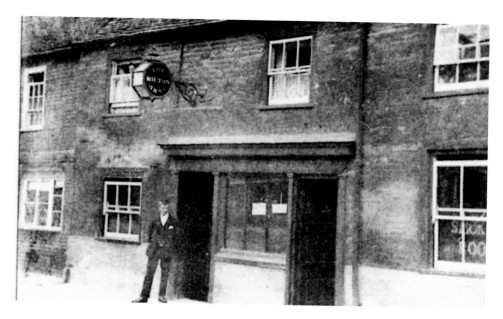

The Wilton Arms

The Wilton Arms, during the late 1800s, was a popular public house situated in West Street. It did a good trade, especially with travellers passing thorough the town, both from and to the West Country. Today this establishment is known as the Bear Inn. The modern day sign however, hangs from the same place as the previous one. The second door nearest the camera has been removed and the window now extended by two more panes of glass. The gentleman in the picture above might well have been the landlord at the time.

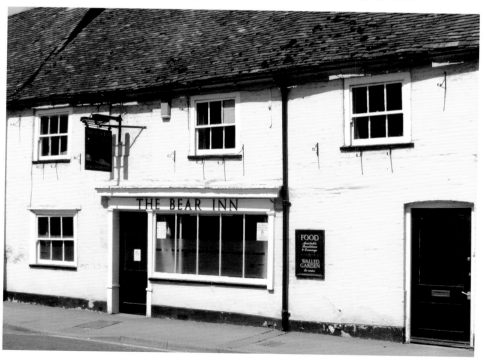

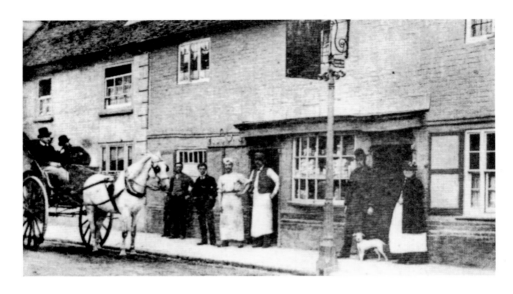

New Inn West Street, c. 1890.

In 1912, when Henry Street was the proprietor, (the father of A. G. Street farmer and broadcaster) he made a third successful application for a billiard licence at Salisbury Licensing Sessions. Street's family had owned the premises since about 1842; Henry was born there not long after. Not being content just to run a pub, he also ran a bakery and grocery from the premises. Today, the building to the left is a 'deli' and the other building now a wine shop and off licence, not all that far removed from its previous existence as a pub. Since the preparation of this book Threshers has closed.

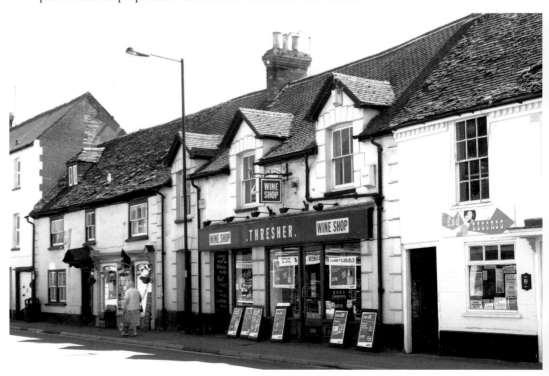

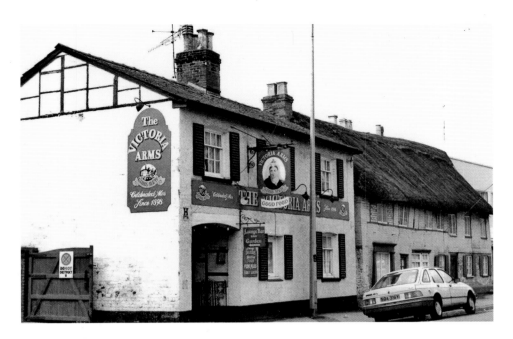

The Victoria Arms

The Victoria Arms in West Street was a very popular pub in its heyday, with both Doris and her husband Fred Payne as its landlords for a number of years. A photograph that was taken in the 1950s has a scribble in pencil on the back, which reads: 'beer about 1s, 3d – 1s 6d a pint'; with today's valuation this is in the region of seven and a half pence. Unfortunately, the pub closed down in the late 1990s and the premises are now owned by the Salisbury Salvage and Demolition Company, who run a successful business selling many popular reclaimed items.

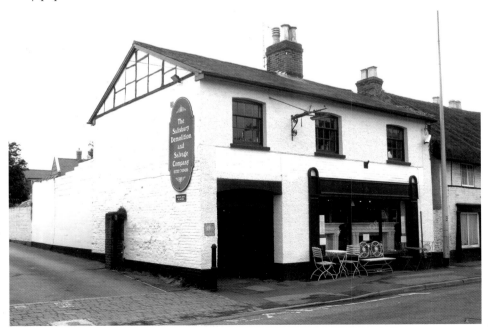

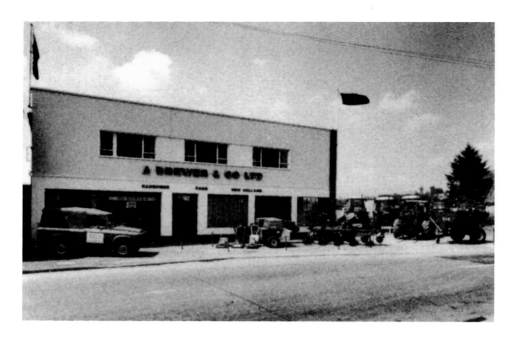

Albert Brewer

It was during the 1860s that a certain Albert Brewer came to work at the felt mills, but he soon set up his own business in West Street as an agricultural engineer. The business proved to be very successful, the workmanship being of a very high standard. It remained under the ownership of the Brewer family until 1912, when the business was sold. The business continued in the old traditions, until eventually it couldn't survive, and went into liquidation in 1985. The premises were transformed into a car sales showroom, then eventually the site was purchased by a property developer and transformed into retirement homes.

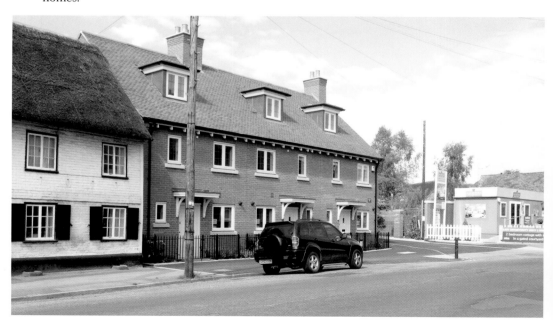

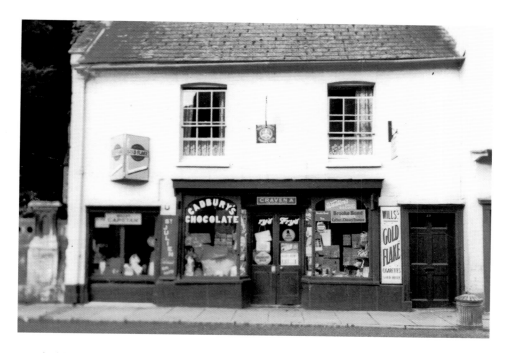

Rumbold's Confectioners and Tobacconist Shop

One of the main features of West Street was Rumbold's. It was an Aladdin's cave of sweets and chocolates, and a great favourite place for children to spend their pennies on a great assortment of treats etc, when rationing ceased after the Second World War. Also sold were small grocery items, and they also did a roaring trade from the workers at Brewers, which was within easy reach. Alas, this shop is no longer there, but it is still often talked about by older generations.

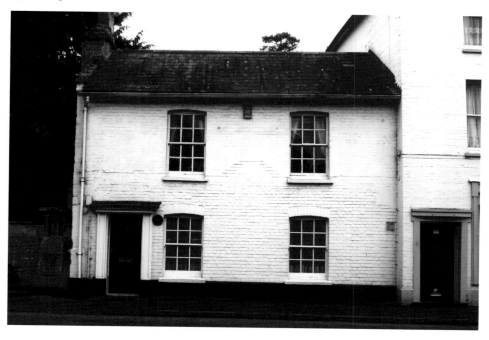

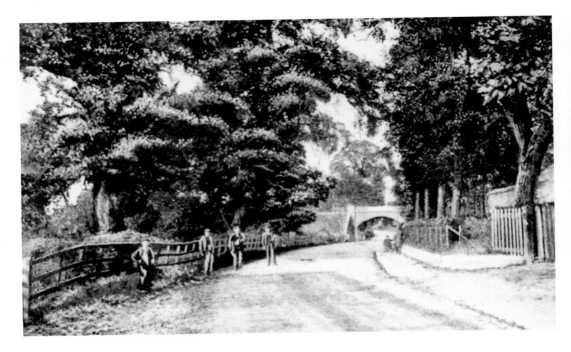

Warminster Road

This idyllic scene above, caught by the cameraman in the second half of the 1800s, today is a busy trunk route of the notorious A36, at the start of the Warminster Road. Not a car is in sight, a rare event in the twenty-first century. The railway bridge in the background at the time was carrying the main London & South Western Railway line to Exeter and the West Country. Today the bridge is still carrying the line, but now just after the former Wilton South Station, it changes from a double to single line operation on the route, with occasional double line passing points.

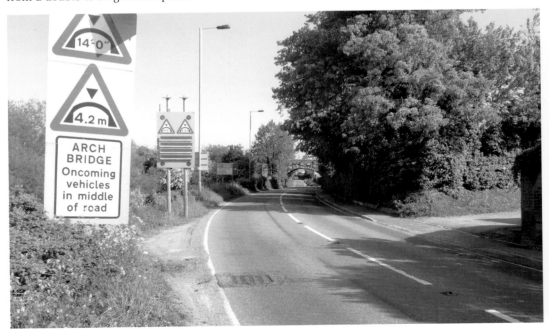

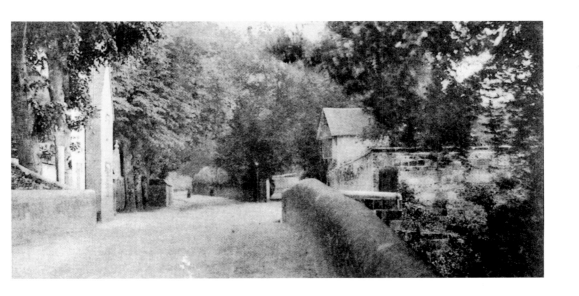

Bulbridge Bridge over the River Nadder

The bridge above was, in a sense, a type of boundary between Wilton and the Bulbridge area of the town of years ago. The photograph was taken in the early 1900s, and the buildings on both sides are still evident today. The development of the Bulbridge housing estate in the early 1970s, and the introduction of a bus service, led to the bridge having to be widened considerably, as shown below.

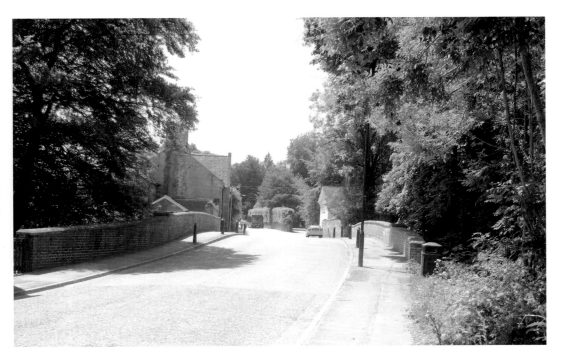

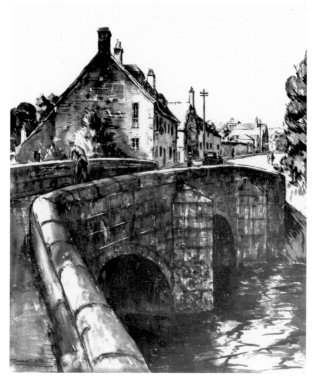

Bulbridge Bridge design

The date of the above drawing of the Bulbridge Bridge, looking towards the town, is not known. However, it does give a good idea of its design in these early times, and is also a tribute to its builders. In fact, when the bridge was actually widened, the old foundations were left in position, as this helped to cut costs. The majority of the new foundations were on either side, with the originals left in the centre portion.

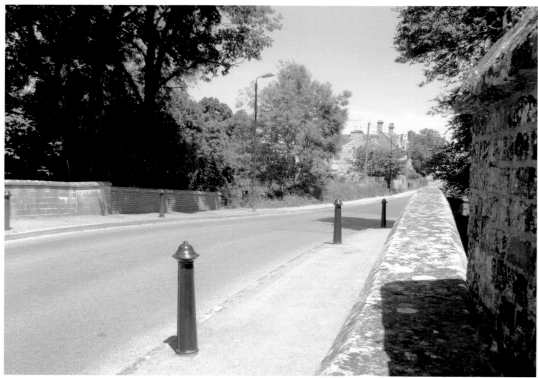

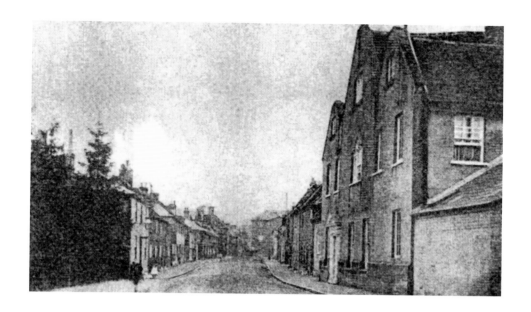

South Street early 1900s

This view of South Street looking towards the town centre was taken before 1919, as the Wool Loft as it was known, is still *in situ*. During the First World War the building was used by the military authorities for storage purposes. It was demolished after the First World War.

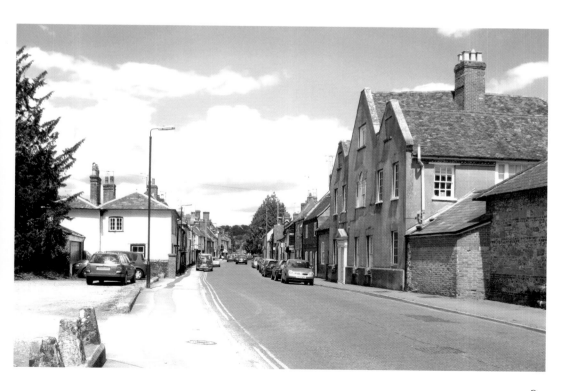

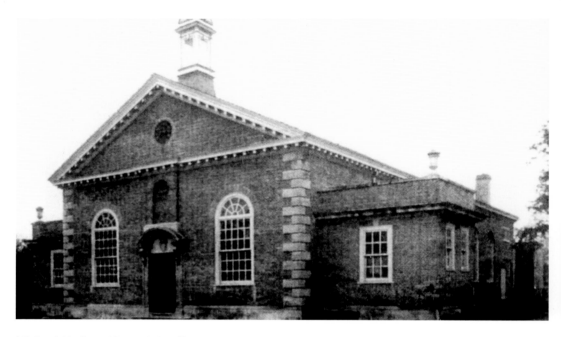

Michael Herbert Memorial Hall

Completed in 1938, this hall was built as a venue for social functions. It was a multi-purpose hall, with a good stage which was used by local drama groups, and it even had a small projection room, so as films could be shown if required. It was also a popular venue for dances on Saturday nights, the regular band being Charles S. Hart and his Orchestra, and a popular band from Salisbury, 'The Merry Macs'. The hall is still in use today, but long gone now are the Saturday night dances of the 1950s and '60s.

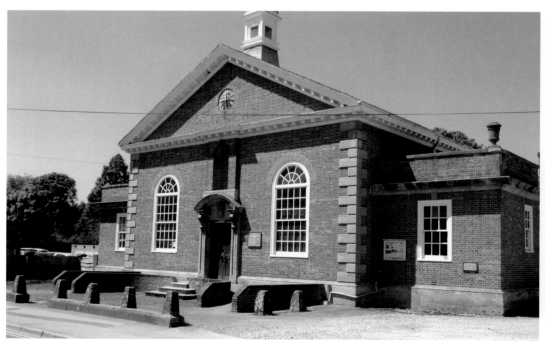

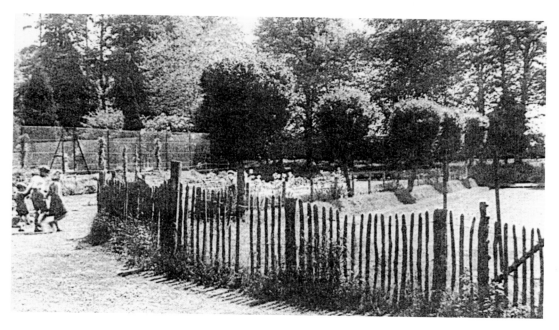

Recreation Ground

This was opened by Lord Pembroke in May 1912, as he had donated the land to the town, being in no further need of it. Lord Pembroke said in his speech that he hoped the area would be well used by all the people of the town. Not only had Lord Pembroke donated the ground, he also loaned Mr Challis, his head gardener, to plan the ground with gardens and supplied many of the plants. The top photograph was taken in the 1950s, and its looks as if the three children passing between the bowling green and the tennis court, are making their way home playing in the grounds, on a lovely summer's day.

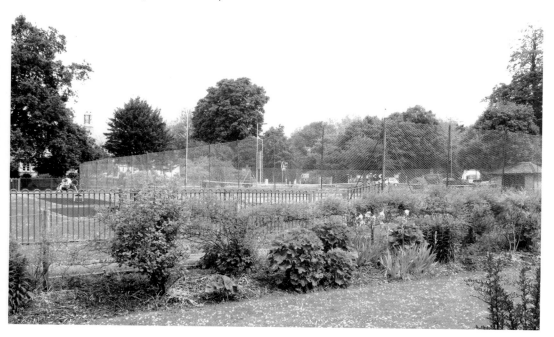

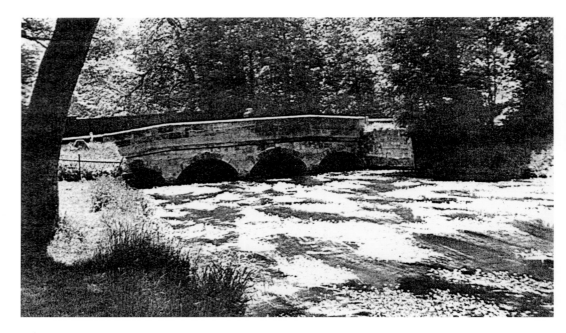

The River Wylye passing the Recreation Ground

Here is a popular spot for people to sit and watch the world go by. The wall in the background separates the grounds of Wilton House from the busy A30 road which passes over the bridge. Due to increaing traffic passing over it in modern times, it had to be strengthened a few years ago, as it was in danger of collapsing. This area is now the home of the drinking fountain, which at one time stood at the bottom of the Avenue, as shown in a previous illustration. Although there is a pipe into the river, unfortunately the fountain, at the time of writing, is still not in working order.

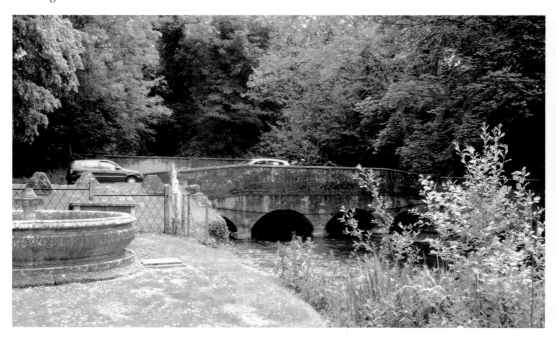

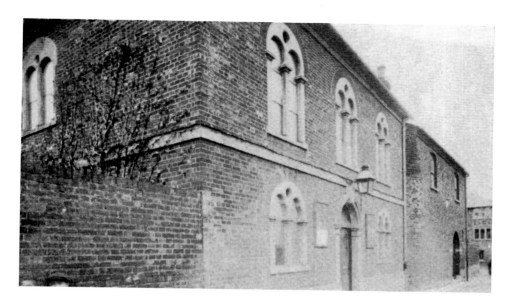

The Congregational Church in Crow Lane

This was erected in 1791, replacing an original chapel on the site, which had become too small for the increasing congregation. The church even had its own graveyard, situated behind the wall to the left of the building. Adjoining the church, in the above photograph, is the vestry on the ground floor, and the upper storey housed the room used as a Sunday School. In the 1980s the church was declared unsafe, and closed down.

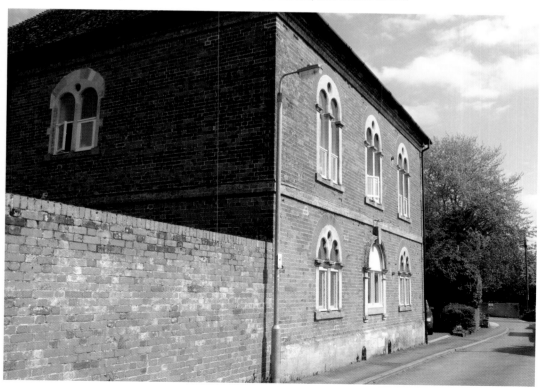

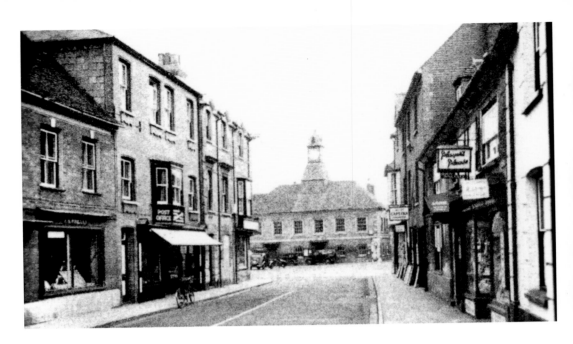

West Street 1950s

The above view looks towards the Town Hall and the market place. On the immediate left is Francis Pretty's iron business, a shop in which all types of tools and accessories to the trade were sold, and where you bought nails by the pound in weight. Next door was the post office, with the shop beyond being Redwoods Grocery Stores. Today, Pretty's is a hardware store, with Reeve the baker, and next door the post office is now the pet shop and Redwoods is now the former HSBC Bank. The former Town Hall is now the Baptist Church. On the right, Snoad's the tobacconist and confectioner is now a 'deli' and Winter's newsagents is now a chiropractors.

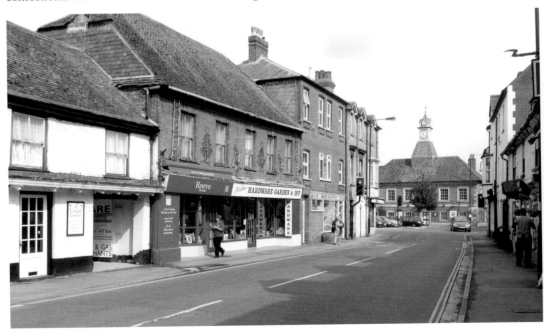

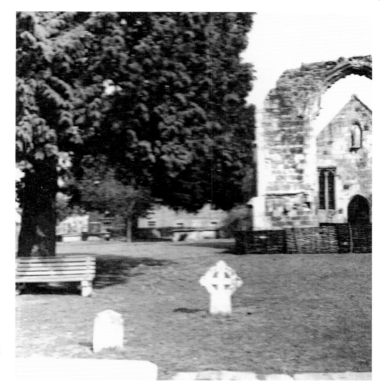

St Mary's Church
Here is a photograph
of St. Mary's church
in the Market Place
back in the early 1950s.
Below shows the view
as it was taken in June
2009. One wonders what
the changes will be in
another fifty years time.

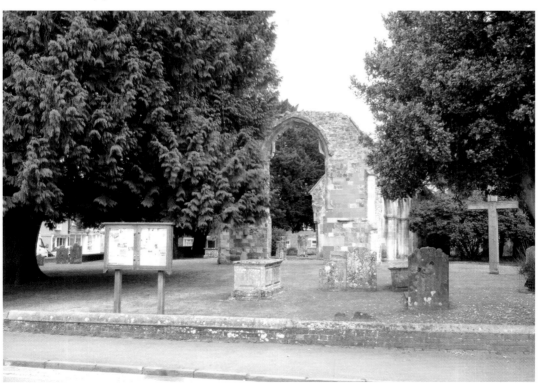

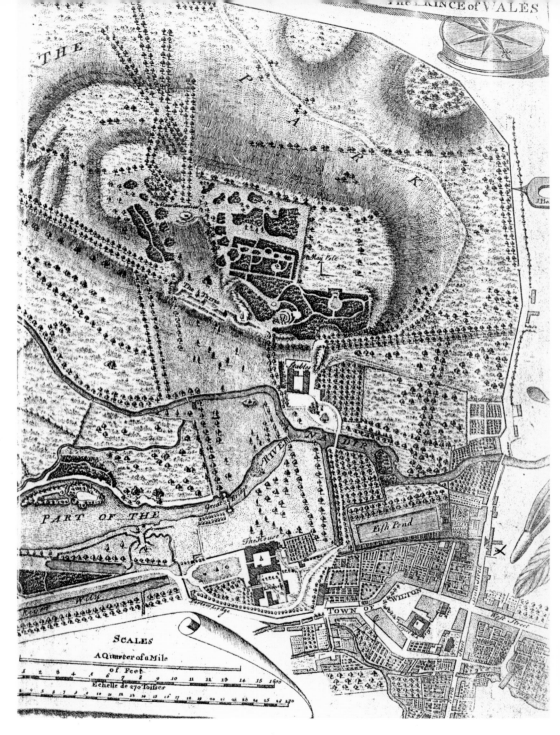

A map dated 1754, showing the part of the Earl of Pembroke's estate known as Wilton Park. To the bottom right is the town centre, showing the Market Place and the carpet factory that was there at the time. The narrow road leading from the market to Kingsbury Square is clearly shown as Carpet Walk.

Wilton Dairy,

→❋ KINGSBURY SQUARE, WILTON. ❋←

(Entrance in Greyhound Lane.)

ARTHUR GARLAND, *Proprietor.*

MILK, CREAM, BUTTER, AND EGGS FRESH DAILY.

FAMILIES WAITED ON TWICE DAILY.

ALL ORDERS RECEIVE PROMPT AND PERSONAL
ATTENTION.

POULTRY TO ORDER   A TRIAL ORDER SOLICITED.

J. SHERGOLD,

Jobbing ⚘ Gardener, ⚘ Florist, ⚘ &c.,

Burdensball, WILTON.

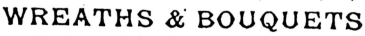

WREATHS & BOUQUETS

Made to order at Moderate Charges.

→❋ CONFECTIONERY. ❋←

TOMATOES GROWN.   **Fire Logs for Sale.**

F. W. MARKS

(Late E. SLOW)

Carriage Builder

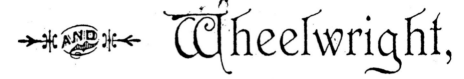 **AND** # Wheelwright,

West End, WILTON,

WILTS.

CARRIAGES BOUGHT OR SOLD ON COMMISSION.

Repairs Neatly Executed.

PAINTING, REPAIRING,

And every description of work connected with the Trade

Executed on the Premises.

PERSONALLY SUPERINTENDED.

ESTIMATES GIVEN.